GW00501993

What it Will Look Like
How leaving the EU and the Single Market can be made to work for Britain

With thanks for research and advice from Robert Oulds,
Gary Robinson and Dr Lee Rotherham

Published in 2017 by
The Bruges Group, 214 Linen Hall, 162-168 Regent Street, London W1B 5TB
www.brugesgroup.com

Follow us on twitter @brugesgroup Find our facebook group: The Bruges Group

Table of Contents

Executive Summary 5

Introduction 7

    The political level 8

Concern one – 'The EU will refuse to give us a deal' (or delay it)...9

    Would a deal need unanimity? Delays to reaching a deal? 12

    Red lines...13

    Ratification failures 13

    How long would an agreement take? 15

Concern Two - 'The UK will have no input in EU decision making' 15

    No Commissioner, No MEPs, No Head of Government at European Council meetings 15

    Why would we want input into EU decision making?..16

    World Trade Organisation 16

    General Agreement on Trade in Services (GATS)..17

    General Agreement on Tariffs and Trade (GATT) 17

    The Technical Barriers to Trade Agreement (TBT)...13

Concern three -The EU will impose punishing tariffs 20

Concern four: Exporting to the EU from outside is not bureaucracy free................................21

    The VAT hurdle...21

    The trade issues which must be solved by David Davis' Brexit Department 22

    Designated port of entry..22

Concern five: There will be complex new 'rules of origin' and

additional paperwork for British goods...24

Concern six: UK businesses will face barriers from accessing EU financial markets..............27

Concern seven: The EU will try to stop the UK accessing EU-third country trade deals........32

Concern eight – The EU will demand access to our fishing waters...34

Concern nine: Security co-operation and cross-border Crime prevention 37

    Extradition...38

Concern ten: Agriculture and EU protectionism and environmental matters...........................39

    Environmental matters..40

Conclusion 41

    WTO Agreement on Trade Facilitation (TFA) 41

    The EEA is not the answer on its own 46

    Gateway Britain 46

The strength of the UK's negotiating position 47

    The Good deal/Bad deal paradox..47

    Self-fulfilling Prophecies 48

    Final words 48

APPENDIX 50

MoUs – the key to a smooth Brexit? 50

Memorandum of Understanding 51

Duration and Term 51

Memorandum of Understanding on Trade and co-operation between
the United Kingdom and the EU and EEA 51

Chapter I: Article 1 Definitions 52

Article 2 Objectives 53

Article 3 Relation to the WTO Agreement and other agreements 53

Article 4 Customs duties 53

Article 5 Joint Committee - establishment 53

Article 6 Joint Committee - constitution 54

Article 7 Political dialogue 54

Article 7 Combating crime and terrorism 54

Article 8 Facilitating trade 55

Final Clauses 55

Authentic texts 55

Executive Summary

Do the advocates of the UK continuing in the European Economic Area, who fear losing participation in the EU's single market, have legitimate concerns? This report will outline how Brexit can be made to work without the safety blanket of the single market, and how many potential issues can be mitigated, and even eliminated altogether, turning them to Britain's advantage.

Brexit negotiations must aim to prevent the complexities of trade slowing the free flow of goods and services after Britain leaves the EU. Any withdrawal agreement between the EU and the UK, must look at these complexities and find practical solutions to make sure that trade enters the EU as seamlessly as possible, and vice-versa.

This report clearly explains how:

There is no such thing as a truly 'Hard Brexit' - but there are significant obstacles.

A UK-EU trade agreement, focused on tariff reduction and clearing customs, could take just 18 months to complete.

The UK's bargaining position is stronger than many commentators believe.

The ten main concerns are usually linked to the following subjects:

The EU will refuse to give us a deal (or delay it)
The EU's treaties themselves advocate for the EU to sign up to free and fair trade arrangements, especially with neighbouring countries.

The UK will have no input in EU decision making
Through the UK going global, and working through the myriad of UN agencies, an outward looking Britain can replace our limited influence in the EU with up-stream influence at the true top tables of world affairs. Setting the agenda at bodies such as the World Trade Organisation.

The EU will impose punishing tariffs
We can be reasonably sure that businesses on the continent will pressure their own governments to reach a deal. Furthermore, global bodies can stop EU protectionism and any prejudice against British producers. Unlike a new trade agreement with a third country, there would be greater pressure for all sides to complete the agreement as soon as possible. While a theoretical new FTA with a third country is likely to create new jobs and profits in the EU, the failure to sign a FTA with the UK would have some adverse effect on jobs and businesses in the remaining EU.

Exporting to the EU from outside is not bureaucracy free
The EU regularly reaches agreements with countries around the globe on reducing red-tape, making it easier to export to the EU. The WTO and World Customs Union are setting the rules which make this even easier.

There will be complex new 'rules of origin' and additional paperwork for British goods

Even Brussels wants to move away from outdated and too stringent customs rules. As supply chains are becoming increasingly globalised the need to demonstrate an item's origins creates a burden for the importer. The need to go through these hoops is becoming anathema even to the EU.

6. **UK businesses will face barriers from accessing EU financial markets**

EU financial regulation allows for third countries to access the European Union market. Companies from countries such as the USA, Hong Kong and Singapore, whose financial regulatory systems are deemed to have 'regulatory equivalence' with the EU, as would the UK, have access to the EU's market in financial services. Increasingly the rules are being set by the WTO, OECD, IMF, the Bank of International Settlements, and the Financial Stability Board to name but a few. Not by Brussels. Furthermore, the EU is involved in international agreements that will open-up the service industry

7. **The EU will try to stop the UK accessing EU-third country trade deals**

The very worst case scenario is that the UK and the country outside the EU that has a trade agreement with the European Union just need to deposit notification, with the UN, or just inform the other parties, that the trade treaties will continue and apply to the UK after our secession. In other words, all these trade treaties don't need to be renegotiated by an independent Britain. Trade with other nations around the globe will continue as before.

8. **The EU will demand access to our fishing waters**

Foreign fleets do not have the right to exploit the UK's Exclusive Economic Zone (EEZ) regime, which is from 12 miles up to 200 miles, or the median line from Britain's shores to those of another state. By accepting this policy, other EU coastal States have given up any claims they may have had, with regard to fishing in what will become the UK's waters. There is no provision for historic rights under international law on fisheries for the fishing limits from 12 to the 200-mile limit. However, the Government and Parliament must not put into domestic law the EU's Common Fisheries Policy. The UK must also withdraw from the 1964 London Convention.

9. **Security co-operation and cross-border Crime prevention**

Additional cross-border crime prevention efforts can be conducted via the International Criminal Police Organisation INTERPOL, the Organization for Security and Co-operation in Europe (OSCE) and the United Nations Office on Drugs and Crime (UNODC). The UK should not seek to retain access to participation in the European Arrest Warrant (EAW). Even without a new extradition treaty the previous arrangements between the UK and the individual EU member states will apply.

10 **Agriculture and EU protectionism and environmental matters**

Leaving the EU will allow Britain to end inappropriate EU laws, such as, stopping the transfer of whale product through UK ports such as Southampton. Britain will also be able to end the export of live animals across the channel for slaughter. The UK should then work through global bodies, such as the Codex Alimentarius Commission to set policy on food and its production.

Britain obtaining tariff free access to the remainder of the EU, along with measures designed to speed the passage of goods through customs, and developing trade links with the third countries around the world will benefit Britain. Having a more liberal regulatory regime and tariff free access to the EU's single market will make the UK a base from which third country producers, who have entered preferential trade deals with Britain, can access the EU without being subject to tariffs. This will make the UK a global trade hub

Introduction

Membership of the single market has; in the opinion of many of those who backed remain in the referendum, totemic importance. Remaining a part of the European Economic Area (EEA), as it is also known, is one of the options considered as an alternative to EU membership. However, it is an alternative that is becoming increasingly unpalatable to many leavers; even those at the top of the British government which once lauded membership of Brussels' internal market.

Supporters of remaining in the European Economic Area, an agreement between the EU and the European Free Trade Association, claim that it is essential for trade to continue unimpeded. There are indeed a number of benefits. The EU's internal market, open to the EFTA states of Iceland, Liechtenstein and Norway, have sought to ease trade by implementing the European Economic Area agreement.

Beyond granting the theoretical access to the single market in services and the right to bid for public procurement, the EEA removes tariff barriers to trade in all areas bar agriculture and fishing. It also attempts to remove all technical barriers to trade. There is regulatory conformity and most importantly the European Economic Area has the mutual recognition of standards. Regulation EC 764/2008 of 9th July 2008 demands that all members allow goods that are legally sold in one country to be sold in another EEA state.

One of the main benefits of being part of the single market comes through the principle of mutual recognition. This allows businesses to export to the entire EU, plus Norway, Iceland and Liechtenstein; the European Economic Area. This is achieved without having to seek standards approval. As the single market is still not complete some member states still have differing demands particularly in the services industry. The principle of mutual recognition is that if a product has been approved as safe and saleable in one member state then it can be sold in all. This bypasses potentially costly and time consuming safety and regulatory checks in each country.

Due to recent ministerial comments, it looks increasingly unlikely that the UK will remain in the single market. This is despite the Liechtenstein model, one of restricting immigration whilst having full access to the single market, as first advocated by the Bruges Group in 2013, and widely publicised by numerous organisations. These range from the Bruges Group to *Flexcit* and the Institute of Economic Affairs[1] where Robert Oulds wrote;

> 'Liechtenstein, an EEA member with less potential influence than Britain, continues to use clauses in the EEA agreement to restrict the movement of persons. Article 112(1) of the EEA Agreement reads: 'If serious economic, societal or environmental difficulties of a sectorial or regional nature liable to persist are arising, a Contracting Party may unilaterally take appropriate measures under the conditions and procedures laid down in Article 113.' The restrictions used by Liechtenstein are further reinforced by Protocol 15 (Articles 5–7) of the EEA agreement. This allows Liechtenstein to keep specific restrictions on the free movement of people. These have been kept in place by what is known as the EEA Council.'

> (EEA Council Decision No. 1/95, Official Journal of the European Communities, 20 April 1995, pages L 86/58 and 86/80).

Rejecting the European Economic Area means an exit where Britain is outside both the EU and the single market. This must be made to work and alternative arrangements will need to be put in place.

---

1   https://iea.org.uk/wp-content/uploads/2016/07/Brexit-interactive.pdf

Yet, do the advocates of the UK continuing in the European Economic Area, who fear losing participation in the EU's internal market, have legitimate concerns?

This report will outline how Brexit can be made to be a great success without the safety blanket of the single market, and how many potential issues can be mitigated, and even eliminated altogether and turned to Britain's advantage.

The Political Level

A deal, if any, on the post-membership arrangement between Britain and the remainder of the EU will at the first instance be agreed at the level of the European Council, comprising the heads of government of the member states. The UK being represented by the Prime Minister.

British Prime Minister Theresa May recently said about a future Brexit deal:

> "I want that deal to reflect the kind of mature, cooperative relationship that close friends and allies enjoy. I want it to include cooperation on law enforcement and counter-terrorism work. I want it to involve free trade, in goods and services. I want it to give British companies the maximum freedom to trade with and operate in the Single Market – and let European businesses do the same here."[2]

Several European leaders[3] have said that they could deny the UK full participation in the single market if the UK does not agree to certain requests – such as maintaining free movement of people or financial contributions.

"There must be a threat, there must be a risk, there must be a price, otherwise we will be in negotiations that will not end well and, inevitably, will have economic and human consequences," the then French President François Hollande said recently.[4]

But what would 'denying the UK participation in the Single Market' actually look like?

Literally speaking, 'denying us access' to the single market would be a trade embargo, which of course simply won't happen.

This is 2017, not the Wild West or the 18th Century. We will not see EU gunboats guarding European ports from British merchant ships and we are unlikely to see costly tariff/customs wars.

As Secretary of State for Exiting the European Union David Davis MP said recently:

> "The damage done by a supposed 'punishment strategy' would be primarily to the industries and farmers on the continent who export to this country.
>
> I'm afraid that Mr Hollande and Madame Merkel and others will find they have pressure back from their own constituents that says this is not a good strategy to pursue."[5]

And as a recent report by the Civitas think-tank stated:

---

2   http://www.independent.co.uk/news/uk/politics/theresa-may-hard-brexit-soft-article-free-movement-deal-single-market-access-a7341886.html

3   https://www.theguardian.com/politics/2016/oct/05/angela-merkel-takes-significantly-tougher-brexit-stance?CMP=Share_iOSApp_Other

4   https://www.theguardian.com/politics/2016/oct/07/uk-must-pay-price-for-brexit-says-francois-hollande

5   https://www.theguardian.com/politics/2016/oct/10/tory-mps-clamour-for-more-say-as-davis-rules-out-vote-on-brexit-terms

'Whereas 3.6 million UK jobs are linked with exports to the EU, 5.8 million EU jobs (excluding the UK) are linked with EU exports to the UK.'[6]

So realistically then, what precisely could the EU do to punish or exclude us and how?

The main concerns are usually linked to the following subjects:

1. The EU will refuse to give us a deal (or delay it)
2. The UK will have no input in EU decision making
3. The EU will impose punishing tariffs
4. Exporting to the EU from outside is not bureaucracy free
5. There will be complex new 'rules of origin' and additional paperwork for British goods
6. UK businesses will face barriers from accessing EU financial markets
7. The EU will try to stop the UK accessing EU-third country trade deals
8. The EU will demand access to our fishing waters
9. Security co-operation and cross-border Crime prevention
10. Agriculture and EU protectionism and environmental matters

Concern one:
'The EU will refuse to give us a deal' (or delay it)

The first worry people have is that the EU will not sign a free trade deal with the UK.

Article 50, the EU's 'exit clause' hints that the EU *should* sign one, but of course it is open to interpretation:

'1. Any Member State may decide to withdraw from the Union in accordance with its own constitutional requirements.

2. A Member State which decides to withdraw shall notify the European Council of its intention. In the light of the guidelines provided by the European Council, the Union shall negotiate and conclude an agreement with that State, setting out the arrangements for its withdrawal, taking account of the framework for its future relationship with the Union. That agreement shall be negotiated in accordance with Article 218(3) of the Treaty on the Functioning of the European Union. It shall be concluded on behalf of the Union by the Council, acting by a qualified majority, after obtaining the consent of the European Parliament.

3. The Treaties shall cease to apply to the State in question from the date of entry into force of the withdrawal agreement or, failing that, two years after the notification referred to in paragraph 2, unless the European Council, in agreement with the Member State concerned, unanimously decides to extend this period.

4. For the purposes of paragraphs 2 and 3, the member of the European Council or of the Council representing the withdrawing Member State shall not participate in the discussions of the European Council or Council or in decisions concerning it.

---

6   http://www.civitas.org.uk/content/files/ukeutradeandjobslinkedtoexports.pdf

A qualified majority shall be defined in accordance with Article 238(3)(b) of the Treaty on the Functioning of the European Union.

5. If a State which has withdrawn from the Union asks to rejoin, its request shall be subject to the procedure referred to in Article 49.'

But aside from Article 50, is there anything else in the EU treaties that might have bearing on a possible deal?

1. In the EU treaties - common provisions, Article 3.5 it reads:

   'In its relations with the wider world, the Union shall…contribute to peace, security…free and fair trade…'

2. In the EU treaties - common provisions, Article 8.1 it reads:

   'The Union shall develop a special relationship with neighbouring countries, aiming to establish an area of prosperity and good neighbourliness, founded on the values of the Union and characterised by close and peaceful relations based on cooperation.'

3. In the EU treaties – Provisions having general application, Article 21 reads:

   'The Union shall seek to develop relations and build partnerships with third countries… The Union shall…work for a high degree of cooperation in all fields of international relations…in order to encourage the integration of all countries into the world economy, including through the progressive abolition of restrictions on international trade.'

4. In the EU treaties – Provisions on the institutions, Article 17 states:

   'The Commission…shall ensure the application of the Treaties.'

When we take these articles together, they tell us that the treaties themselves advocate for the EU to sign up to free and fair trade arrangements, especially with neighbouring countries, and that the European Commission is supposed to enforce the *application* of the treaties.

EU researcher Dr Richard North has stated on this subject that:

'European Union negotiators must, therefore, entertain reasonable attempts to reduce trade restrictions, in accordance with treaty provisions. Moreover, their actions are justiciable. If EU negotiators departed from these legal provisions, or if they or any member states sought to impose trade restrictions or other sanctions in order to increase leverage, the UK would have the option of lodging a complaint with the European Court of Justice (ECJ)'[7]

In addition to these points, we can be reasonably sure that businesses on the continent will pressure their own governments to reach a deal. If we look at Germany specifically:

Markus Kerber, the head of the BDI, which represents German industry said to the BBC before the EU referendum that it would be *"very, very foolish"* if the EU imposed trade barriers on the UK when it leaves the EU.[8]

He also said that,

"Imposing trade barriers, imposing protectionist measures between our two countries - or between the two political centres, the European Union on the one hand and the UK on the other - would be a

---

7   Flexcit, Pg 37

8   http://www.bbc.co.uk/news/business-36596060

very, very foolish thing in the 21st Century… The BDI would urge politicians on both sides to come up with a trade regime that enables us to uphold and maintain the levels of trade we have."

Speaking after the Brexit vote, Dr Jens Weidmann President of the Deutsche Bundesbank (who also sits on the ECB's governing council) said:

"For the first time in the history of European integration, a country wishes to leave the EU. This decision is very regrettable and, in my eyes, a mistake. But it should be respected and we will have to deal with it.

"It is in the interests of both parties for the EU and the United Kingdom to quickly enter into level-headed negotiations on their future relationship. Neither party will have anything to gain from erecting trade barriers…the UK is Germany's third most important export destination."[9]

These comments echo those by Michael Roth, Germany's European Affairs minister who has said:

"Given Britain's size, significance and its long membership of the European Union, there will probably be a special status which only bears limited comparison to that of countries that have never belonged to the European Union. I want relations between the European Union and Britain to be as close as possible"

Mr Roth has also stated that: *"Britain is a major economy and has been an EU member for decades. We will surely reach a custom-fit agreement between the EU and Britain."[10]*

German Economy Minister Sigmar Gabriel said recently: *"My personal point of view is: We should do everything, as far as this is politically justifiable, to keep the Britons as close as possible to Europe"[11]*

Ilse Aigner, the Bavarian economy minister was quoted by Die Welt as saying that:

"Great Britain is one of the most important trading partners of Bavaria…we must do our utmost to eliminate the uncertainties that have arisen.

There must be ways to re-establish economic relations with Great Britain without interruption."[12]

And as the German business Journalist Wolfgang Münchau wrote recently:

"I was looking at UK-German trade data and found something that surprised me. Germany is not only exporting more goods to the UK, which we knew; it also has a surplus in services, including finance, according to the Federal Statistics Office. UK services exports to Germany were €24bn in 2015, while the UK imported services of €41bn from Germany.

"If a hard Brexit were to force the UK and the EU to impose quotas on traded goods and to suspend trade in most services, Germany would be harder hit than the UK."[13]

So to recap then, if the EU were to not reach a free trade deal with the UK, it could be considered to be acting in contravention of its own rules and would be ignoring the advice of many senior German figures.

---

9   https://www.bundesbank.de/Redaktion/EN/Reden/2016/2016_07_01_weidmann.html#doc372730bodyText4

10   http://www.bloomberg.com/news/articles/2016-08-17/germany-sees-tailor-made-brexit-deal-as-u-k-tests-patience-irzfynyf

11   http://www.reuters.com/article/us-britain-eu-germany-idUSKBN13X1E6

12   https://www.welt.de/regionales/bayern/article159718157/Aigner-fuerchtet-Brexit-Folgen-und-fordert-neue-Handelsabkommen.html

13   https://www.ft.com/content/1394c4da-97a7-11e6-a1dc-bdf38d484582

Would a deal need unanimity? Delays to reaching a deal?

Some commentators have suggested that even if the EU and key countries like Germany took a pragmatic approach and wished to offer the UK a trade deal, the deal could be vetoed by one or more countries wishing to either punish the UK or extract specific concessions.

This would depend largely on the timing and complexity of the deal struck, and whether it was concluded inside the two-year Article 50 process.

If the deal was a straightforward one under Article 50, the decision would be taken by qualified majority voting. This would need the approval of the European Parliament but no individual country would have a veto. Nor is it subject to ratification by national parliaments.

However, a more complex arrangement could require ratification by member states as well as the European Parliament. Under such a process reaching a more complex deal could take much longer before it comes into force.

Article 50 does allow for negotiations to be extended if necessary, however that is politically and practically untenable. A government delaying Brexit is risking its own future. What is more, the UK would need to withdraw before the 2019 European elections and the formation of a new European Commission. A transitional arrangement in which the UK remains a part of the EEA (European Economic Area) until the ink is dry on new agreements could be concluded if necessary. Yet, that is anathema to many.

Have no doubt, a deal will be concluded without any period of interruption – few EU countries could absorb the costs and loss of jobs that would result from new trade barriers with the UK.

The EU itself is reeling from problems with the Eurozone, migration problems, high unemployment, border issues and tensions with Russia. In addition, a major net contributor to the EU budget is leaving.

> 'Excluding Germany, Britain's contribution is more than the total net contribution of the 26 other EU states combined. ...add up the debits and credits of every member state from France to Poland bar Germany and it comes to a figure less than Britain's EU contribution. Britain's exit will be a massive budget hit to the EU...'[14]

They simply cannot afford to 'make an example' of the UK – but some countries might still try to squeeze concessions out of the UK with their own 'red lines'.

Red lines

A recent report by the Cicero group[15] looks at most of the concessions and red lines each country might look for in the Brexit negotiations.

Of particular concern is the demands that could be made by the so-called 'Visegrad Group' of countries – the Czech Republic, Hungary, Poland and Slovakia.

In recent years many citizens from those countries have come to live and work in the UK. According to figures cited in a BBC report, there were 831,000 Polish-born residents in the UK in 2015.[16]

---

14   https://order-order.com/2017/01/12/eu-faces-funding-cliff-edge/

15   http://cicero-group.com/wp-content/uploads/2016/10/Brexit-negotiations-The-View-from-the-EU.pdf

16   http://www.bbc.co.uk/news/uk-politics-37183733

It is widely believed that the Visegrad will oppose any arrangement that does not allow their citizens to live and work in the UK after Brexit, although a BBC report[17] in September 2016 suggests their demands only refer to those citizens resident in the UK at the time of the referendum.

Looking after one's citizens is an important duty of a government of course, and that can be understood and respected. However, the UK must be fair but firm with the Visegrad group. We must give them assurances on the rights of their citizens already living and working in the UK.

EU citizens in the UK, and British citizens living abroad in other EU states have made use of the free movement of persons – a right enshrined in EU treaties. Those that have established a residency, which will include both living and owning property, in an EU member state will have their rights protected after withdrawal. This entitlement is known as an 'executed right'. Article 70 b. of the Vienna Convention states that the withdrawal from a treaty 'Does not affect any right, obligation or legal situation of the parties created through the execution of the treaty prior to its termination.'

This view is supported by the constitutional expert Lord McNair. He concluded that such rights established by a treaty will remain in force even if the agreement is terminated by Britain's exit. In law they are considered to be executed by the treaty and 'have an existence independent of it; the termination cannot touch them.' Their status will be guaranteed as a result of the 'well-recognised principle of respect for acquired [vested] rights' (McNair 1961). Furthermore, it is a legal norm, *The Oxford Journal* in its year book on international law argues that Acquired Rights are Customary Law and therefore take precedence over national law at the international level. Furthermore, they will be regarded as such by the International Court of Justice in the Hague. Therefore Britain leaving the EU will have no impact on EU citizens already resident here or for British citizens living abroad.

Yet it must be made clear to the Visegrad group that we are leaving the EU and so freedom of movement cannot continue as before. We can point to the fact that the UK has a large trade deficit with the Visegrad countries and so it is in everyone's best interest for the UK's departure to be as smooth as possible, with a future relationship based on friendship, free trade and mutual defence.

Ratification failures

So far, the EU has failed to conclude the Trans-Atlantic Trade and Investment Partnership (TTIP) and has had great difficulty in ratifying the CETA agreement with Canada. If the EU also failed to conclude a deal with the UK, it would further damage the EU's credibility on the international scene.

Unlike TTIP and CETA, which are new trade arrangements with third countries, a UK-EU free trade deal would be much simpler to agree and implement – since the UK is already 'synchronised' with EU common standards, rules and regulations.

As EU expert Dr Lee Rotherham wrote;

> '…many of the concerns generated by TTIP will simply not be present in any UK-EU 'Channel Treaty'. The very starting point is one of full compliance, rather than finding thousands of points of common ground after decades of variation.

'Newton's First Law of Motion works against advocates of CETA as they seek change against opposing forces (Walloon or otherwise); it also conversely works against those advocating the imposition of tariffs and obstacles on UK trade flows with the continent after Brexit.'[18]

In addition, unlike a new trade agreement with a third country, there would be greater pressure for all sides to complete the agreement as soon as possible. While a theoretical new FTA with a third country is *likely* to create new jobs and profits in the EU, the failure to sign a FTA with the UK definitely *would* have some adverse effect on jobs and businesses in the EU.

These factors would help concentrate minds on the continent and speed up the ratification of a UK-EU deal.

How long would an agreement take?

The former EU Commission who had responsibility for the Internal Market and Services, Michel Barnier has been optimistic. He stated that a deal could be reached by October 2018, approximately 18 months from when the UK aims to submit its withdrawal notice.[19] The European Commission appointed him as their Chief Negotiator in charge of the Preparation and Conduct of the Negotiations with the United Kingdom under Article 50, this is despite the fact that the notice had not then been submitted, and that the ultimate responsibility is with the European Council.

Furthermore, while EU free trade agreements are notoriously long to conclude this has not always been the case. The earlier incarnation of the EU, the European Economic Community (EEC) concluded basic FTAs with Austria, Iceland, Portugal, Sweden and Switzerland in the 1970s in *seven months*. The EEC began negotiations with Norway on a similar FTA in February 1973, which came into force on the first of July 1973 – six months from start to finish.

---

18   Report: *The National Interest* by Dr Lee Rotherham

19   http://www.telegraph.co.uk/news/2016/12/06/eu-brexit-negotiator-michel-barnier-reiterate-no-cherry-picking/

Concern two:
'The UK will have no input in EU decision making'

No Commissioner, No MEPs, No Head of Government at European Council meetings

When the UK leaves the EU, we will of course no longer have a Commissioner in the European Commission.

It is debatable how much of an impact this will really make, since EU commissioners swear an oath to the Union itself, not to the UK[20]:

> "Having been appointed as a Member of the European Commission by the European Council, following the vote of consent by the European Parliament
>
> I solemnly undertake:
>
> - to respect the Treaties and the Charter of Fundamental Rights of the European Union in the fulfilment of all my duties;
>
> - to be completely independent in carrying out my responsibilities, in the general interest of the Union;
>
> - in the performance of my tasks, neither to seek nor to take instructions from any Government or from any other institution, body, office or entity;
>
> - to refrain from any action incompatible with my duties or the performance of my tasks.
>
> I formally note the obligation laid down under the Treaty on the Functioning of the European Union, by virtue of which each Member State is to respect this principle and is not to seek to influence Members of the Commission in the performance of their tasks.
>
> I further undertake to respect, both during and after my term of office, the obligations arising therefrom, and in particular the duty to behave with integrity and discretion as regards the acceptance, after I have ceased to hold office, of certain appointments or benefits."

Additionally, EU Commissioners are reportedly threatened with the loss of their pensions if they are too critical of the EU[21] so really 'our' commissioner cannot plausibly be said to be there to represent British interests, they work for the EU.

The UK will lose its MEPs (Members of the European Parliament) when it leaves the EU; that is true.

The European Parliament has 751 Members, of which just over seventy represent the UK.

However, they are from different parties and make up different political groups inside the European Parliament – the British MEPs do not vote as a bloc and often vote against each other along Eurosceptic, Europhile, socialist, conservative and liberal fault-lines.

---

20   http://europa.eu/rapid/press-release_IP-14-2511_en.htm

21   http://www.telegraph.co.uk/news/politics/labour/4996440/Lord-Mandelson-must-remain-loyal-to-EU-to-guarantee-pension.html

Even if all the UK MEPs did vote as a bloc, they would be roundly outvoted on major issues. So we won't really be losing that much influence when their terms end.

The only real loss then is the fact that the British Prime Minister will not be present at meetings of the European Council.[22]

Post-Brexit, the British Prime Minister will still meet with heads of EU countries at meetings of NATO, the G20 and other international fora; British Ambassadors will still have regular dialogues with European counterparts, UK diplomats will speak to their opposite numbers at the UN and at the Council of Europe. In short then, leaving the EU will not lead to any isolation.

Why would we want input into EU decision making?

Some readers might now be asking themselves – 'why do we even want input into EU rules if we are leaving the EU? We don't have seats in the Chinese National People's Congress or the U.S. House of Representatives?'

While it is true that we are leaving the European Union, they are still going to be our nearest and arguably most important trading partner.

This means that our industries and exporters will want three things:

- To buy and sell with European companies and individuals with as little red tape and tariffs as possible.
- To be kept up to date with the latest European rules and regulations so they can tailor their products to legally be exported to EU countries.
- For the UK government to lobby the EU or influence its rules so that no new measures that harm British business will be introduced.

Before we can address these issues further, we need to look at the history of the EU and its relationship with other international organisations.

The EU's earlier incarnation the EEC (European Economic Community) was set up in the late 1950s, a time in which average tariff levels were high and international trade was a different animal.

The original basic GATT (General Agreement on Tariffs and Trade) agreement had been signed in the previous decade, but all sorts of taxes and non-tariff barriers still hindered trade. So it appeared to make sense for trading nations to club together for mutual benefit.

World Trade Organisation

In 1995, just two years after the Maastricht Treaty came into force, which changed the European Community (EC) into the European Union (EU), another organisation came into existence – the World Trade Organisation or WTO (a newer and more comprehensive iteration of GATT).

As members of the EU, on most issues the EU Trade Commissioner takes the place of national representatives at the WTO.[23]

---

22   http://www.consilium.europa.eu/en/european-council/

23   https://www.wto.org/english/thewto_e/countries_e/european_communities_e.htm

Not only are all EU member states individually signed up to World Trade Organisation rules, but the EU itself is also a member[24].

This means that the EU is signed up to the WTO and GATT agreements, including:

General Agreement on Trade in Services (GATS)[25]

An agreement between WTO members which provides a framework for cross-border services trade.

General Agreement on Tariffs and Trade (GATT)[26]

Which encourages signatories to work together to resolve trade disputes and encourages lower tariffs between members. Provides a framework for cross-border trade in goods.

The Technical Barriers to Trade Agreement (TBT)[27]

The Technical barriers to trade agreement encourages members to work together to reduce non-tariff barriers to trade, such as divergent product standards and regulations.

The WTO website states that:

'…the TBT Agreement includes features specific to the preparation and application of regulatory measures that affect trade in goods: it strongly encourages the use of international standards, and it emphasizes the need to avoid unnecessary barriers to trade. The TBT Agreement is binding on all members of the WTO. The TBT Agreement covers trade in all goods (both agricultural and industrial).'[28]

A College of Europe Report titled 'The Legal Status and Influence of Decisions of International Organizations and other Bodies in the European Union' by Ramses A. Wessel (Professor of International and European Law and Governance) and Steven Blockmans (Professor of EU External Relations Law and Governance) states clearly:

'The influence of the WTO on the EU cannot be understated.

'WTO primary and secondary law have had a considerable influence on EU primary and secondary law and their interpretation.

'Much of the EU's primary law on the free circulation of goods has been inspired by GATT 1947, and the integration of new trade subjects into the WTO 1994 triggered a constitutional process of expanding the EU's exclusive powers concerning commercial policy.

'Moreover, many pieces of secondary EU legislation either transpose WTO norms or have been modified to bring them into line with world trade standards after adverse WTO judicial decisions.'

The report goes on to say that it is not only the WTO that influences EU rules:

---

24   https://www.wto.org/english/thewto_e/countries_e/european_communities_e.htm

25   https://www.wto.org/english/tratop_e/serv_e/gatsqa_e.htm

26   https://www.wto.org/english/docs_e/legal_e/gatt47_e.pdf

27   https://www.wto.org/english/tratop_e/tbt_e/tbt.htm

28   https://www.wto.org/english/res_e/publications_e/tbttotrade_e.pdf

'...rules, standards, codes of conduct, guidelines, principles, recommendations and best practices developed within a variety of international organizations and bodies influence the development of EU law, even if they are not strictly legally binding upon the Union.

'Thus, norms developed within several bodies, be it within the UN family such as the Food and Agriculture Organization (FAO), the Codex Alimentarius Commission and the World Health Organization (WHO), or the OECD, the G20 and some of the machinery this 'international regime' has brought to life, such as the Financial Stability Board (FSB), and specific bodies bringing together financial watchdogs like the Basel Committee on Banking Supervision (BCBS) and the International Organization of Securities Commissions (IOSCO) – have been dealt with within the EU legislature and/or judiciary.'

The EU, however, recognises as part of the case law underpinning the workings of the European Union that international law is to be incorporated into EU law which therefore, via Brussels, becomes the law of each and every member state. The legal decisions of the European Court of Justice which confirm this are: Case 104/81, Kupferberg, Case C-192/89 Sevince and Case C-277/94 Taflan-Met.

Outside the EU, the UK will regain its WTO seat and vote and be an independent voice on these other bodies, since we will no longer be subject to the Articles 24 and 34 of the 'GENERAL PROVISIONS ON THE EUROPEAN UNION'S EXTERNAL ACTION AND SPECIFIC PROVISIONS ON THE COMMON FOREIGN AND SECURITY POLICY'.[29]

A report on this topic by the Eurosceptic group Business for Britain concluded that:

'Increasingly, the WTO and other international bodies have more fundamental significance for UK trade than the EU. Were the UK to regain the right to speak for itself in these organisations, it would be better positioned to exert influence on international trade policy.'

– Business for Britain *Change or Go* report

Thus, while we will not be in the room when EU rules are voted on, the UK will have greater influence on the bodies who shape the international rules that seek to minimise barriers to trade. Instead of being a passive receiver of EU regulation Britain will have up-stream influence.

To make it clear - rules which exporters must abide by are increasingly originating from, and being set at, the international level - not by the European Union.

'The notion that being outside the EU means you don't get to write the rules of world trade is back to front. The EU is increasingly at the mercy of others' rules set at the supranational level anyway: regaining our independence would increase our influence there.'

– Viscount Ridley, writing in *The Times* 20th July 2015

As long as our products meet international standards there is no reason why trade should not continue unabated. And as the UK regains its seat at the WTO it will be able to raise concerns about the EU's behaviour towards it there, if need be.

'The large majority of EU rules are those governing health and safety standards of industrial and food products for consumers and workers, of which about one quarter are international (ISO) standards, these being usually copy-and-paste identical to EU ones.

---

29   http://brexitcentral.com/gary-robinson-brexit-will-allow-uk-regain-distinctive-voice-world-stage/

'So export-oriented UK industries will carry on using the EU standards to win the CE mark...free to adopt their own standards where they think they can meet essential safety standards less expensively.'

– Michael Emerson, Associate Senior Research Fellow at the Centre for European Policy Studies and former EU Ambassador to Moscow

A report by the Adam Smith Institute also expounded on this very subject, stating:

'As more and more issues are addressed at global level, the EU is steadily losing control over its own regulatory agenda. For example, more than 80 percent of the EEA acquis (and therefore the EU's Single Market legislation) falls within the ambit of existing international organisations and is thus potentially amenable to global regulation'.[30]

It is important to bear in mind that until Brexit takes place, the UK is a member of the European single market. As a result, our rules and regulations are already synced with EU/EEA rules and regulations since they largely *are the same* rules.

As a result, we can argue that combined with the WTO agreement on Technical Barriers to Trade (which the EU itself and all EU member states are signed up to) we will have equivalent standards post-Brexit. Trade cannot be legally stopped if British standards meet applicable international standards.

Furthermore, under WTO rules, all countries have to give other WTO members (relatively) free and fair trade - a status called MFN or 'most favoured nation' status.

The head of the World Trade Organisation Roberto Azevedo was interviewed recently on the topic of Brexit[31] - he said:

"I told (Trade Secretary Liam Fox) that I myself and the WTO secretariat will be available to make the transition as smooth as possible.

"They [the UK] have to renegotiate but it does not mean that they are not members. Members renegotiate their commitments all the time – so they will be renegotiating a particular set of commitments that they have now, under the EU - a transition from those commitments to another set of commitments; and trade will not stop, it will continue and members will be negotiating with the UK the legal basis under which that trade is going to happen.

"But it does not mean that you have a vacuum or a 'disruption' in terms of trade flows or anything of the kind – not automatically.

"And we will be working by the way, I myself personally; very intensely to ensure that this transition is fast and is smooth.

"I think the less turbulence the better. The global economy today is not in the best shape for us to be introducing turbulence."

---

30   http://www.adamsmith.org/stuck-in-the-middle-with-eu/

31   http://news.sky.com/story/brexit-will-not-cause-uk-trade-disruption-wto-boss-10632803

Concern three:
The EU will impose punishing tariffs

Currently as a member of the EU we have zero tariffs (customs taxes) with other EU countries.

With a free trade agreement, the UK could maintain a similar tariff arrangement when we leave, it is highly likely that the EU will wish to sign one with us.

Even if we did not manage to sign a FTA with the EU, the European Union would not have *carte blanche* authority to impose whatever tariffs on the UK it wished to impose.

As we have already explored in the previous sections, the UK is a WTO member and a GATT signatory, like the EU itself and all EU member states.

Since the creation of GATT, average tariffs have been dropping fairly steady around the world for decades.

The EU could therefore only subject us to the low MFN or 'most favoured nation' tariff rates. If the EU wished to put punitive taxes on UK exports, they would need to also adjust their tariffs on goods from other major trading partners. Unless this was a temporary safeguarding action, this would also need to be agreed at the WTO.

In a report[32] for the Policy Network think tank by Pat McFadden MP, Labour's Shadow Minister for Europe, he explained that after Brexit, if the UK did not sign a Free Trade Agreement with the UK:

'UK businesses exporting goods and services to EU Member States would be subject to the EU's Common External Tariff. The maximum tariff under WTO are those which the EU currently applies under the general WTO regime. While tariffs would be imposed on roughly 90% of the goods which the UK exports to the EU, on average EU tariffs are low (1%).'

Although tariffs on exports to the EU would be low on average, Mr McFadden makes the point that certain industries would be affected more than others:

'Car exports would be subject to a tariff of 10% and car-parts to a tariff of 5%.'

So while trading with the EU on WTO rates wouldn't be impossible, it would still be wise for the UK to seek a FTA with the EU. The potential extra costs of tariffs placed on British exports to the EU is, however, more than mitigated by the reduction in the value of the pound.

Whilst every possibility exists of there being an agreement(s) on reducing tariffs between the UK and the EU, this does not in itself eliminate all the bureaucratic hurdles.

---

32   http://www.policy-network.net/publications/4995/What-would-out-look-like

Concern four: Exporting to the EU from outside is not bureaucracy free

Exporting into the EU requires a convoluted process to be completed. Goods must have assigned to them an identification number, inputted at the port of destination. The larger exporters find the process easier. They can make their declarations at the end of the month. Those who export less to the EU will, however, be faced with bureaucratic hurdles.

Clearance for use, allowing the product to go into circulation to be sold in the UK, or an EU country, needs to be obtained. The process for assessing this, even in the EU, will differ from country to country. Mostly, however, this is often just a theoretical problem, rarely do customs officials demand compliance with national standards and rarely do they conduct a strict examination of documentation declaring that an item conforms to national or EU standards.[33] It is legally possible to detain goods on the grounds of differing standards, but in practice this only usually applies to items that are deemed to be dangerous, illegal, or subject to anti-dumping duty (a tax on products suspected of being sold substantially below their normal value in the market in which it was produced).

Still, the process of shipping goods to and from the EU is not without other bureaucratic impediments. The freedom of the items is also strictly regulated. Any goods entering the EU, if not cleared at port, which can be a laborious process, must be stored in a bonded warehouse, also known as an Enhanced Remote Transit Shed (ERTS) warehouse. Until they are declared to customs officials for an approved treatment or use.

Transhipped cargo not in free circulation will also require what is known as a CMR document. The CMR is a consignment note with a standard set of transport and liability conditions, which replaces individual businesses' terms and conditions. It confirms that the carrier (i.e. the road haulage company) has received the goods and that a contract of carriage exists between the trader and the carrier. It derives from the Convention on the Contract for the International Carriage of Goods by Road.

The process of clearing customs is increasingly becoming electronic. Systems used by exporters that integrate with the British customs system are the CNS and Destin8 computer systems.

The VAT hurdle

Value Added Tax (VAT) is often charged on imported goods, that is in addition to any customs duties. The details must be entered onto the Customs Handling of Import and Export Freight (CHIEF) system. This system records the declaration to the customs authorities, capturing details of the goods and whether they are transported by land, air and sea entering or leaving the UK/EU. It allows importers, exporters and freight forwarders to complete customs information electronically. This is not without charge.

If there is no prior agreement for each consignment, going to a specific destination, to clear customs the importer must produce customs records for each, pay VAT and the customs duty, if any. This will be calculated per the value of the item at its final point of sale. The VAT rate will differ from country to country, and even item to item. In some cases, a product will be exempt, VAT will not apply. In other cases, an item will be zero-rated, requiring the documentation to be completed but with no final payment. Even where tariffs are eliminated, when importing from outside the EU there is still the requirement to pay

---

33   Primary research with managers in the logistics industry

Value Added Tax. If the exporter is registered for VAT then this can be claimed back but only if they are registered. There is also the requirement for an input VAT certificate to be completed.

Remaining a part of the EU's customs union (having its trade rules apply) without being in the EU, does not eliminate the requirement to complete form filling. The requirement to clear customs and complete documentation, known as an ATA Carnet, to validate the origin of goods and confirm that they are free from tariffs even applies to Turkey. This country is considered a part of the EU's customs union and therefore has tariff free access for industrial products; but it is not bureaucracy free access.[34]

David Davis' Department for Exiting the European Union must focus on addressing the logistical trade hurdles of delays at customs posts. The alternative will be even worse congestion on the M20 after Brexit than that which exists at present.

The trade issues which must be solved by David Davis' Brexit Department

Brexit negotiations must aim to prevent the complexities of trade slowing the free flow of goods after Britain leaves the EU. Any withdrawal agreement between the EU and the UK, must look at these complexities and find practical solutions to make sure that trade enters the EU as seamlessly as possible, and vice-versa.

The biggest challenges to resolve are the practical logistics. Few, if any, so far, have looked at these issues from the perspective of eliminating, or at least mitigating, the real hurdles that would appear after Brexit.

Inside the EU, exporting to Berlin is effectively not any different from sending goods to Birmingham, just that the transportation will, due to the distance involved set a slightly greater logistical challenge. There is no requirement for burdensome bureaucracy when moving goods between EU member states. When goods from Britain are transported to the EU, just like those destined to our shores from the European Union, they come and go via our ports, be they channel ports like Dover or airports such as Heathrow. Presently this is with no let or hindrance. No administration is involved. In fact, national borders in terms of trade can be said to no longer exist within the European Union. At least some red-tape, has been eliminated. Yet, without a practical agreement businesses that are involved in either exporting to the EU, or importing from it, will face costly delays.

The enormous mutual dependency, between British and continental firms, rightly cited by many as a reason why an agreement will eventually be reached on issues such as trade tariffs, have, however, not considered that the high volume of trade can be a source of problems. This centres around the fact that all imports to the EU must go through customs posts.

Designated port of entry

When exporting goods to another territory the host nation can stipulate a designated port of entry for the product. At present Britain and the European Union are one trade zone, the UK has free access to any and all established places where both people and produce can be admitted. The EU has the hypothetical ability in the short term to prescribe ports of entry, and terms, that are inconvenient for British exporters. However, this will be a serious breach of international trade law. Articles XI:1, XIII:1, V:2, V:6 and I:1 of the 1994 General Agreement on Tariffs and Trade now administered by the World Trade Organisation.

---

34   http://eur-lex.europa.eu/LexUriServ/LexUriServ.do?uri=OJ:L:2006:265:0018:0038:en:PDF

Under these rules one country cannot be treated less favourably than any other state in the export and transit of goods. What is more, as both businesses and consumers on the continent depend upon British imports there is no reason to believe that such problems will arise.

Regardless of how the UK leaves the EU it should be business as usual via the existing ports of entry. Indeed, Brexit negotiations should seek to expand them to include more destinations accessible via HS1, the Channel Tunnel.

So far so good. However, there are other serious issues.

The UK's trade in goods with third countries outside the EU is often relatively unfettered because it is in bite-sized portions. The trade from Britain through the many customs posts of the numerous states around the globe to which Britain exports is in manageable quantities. However, the sheer scale of goods going through for instance French ports is staggering. Quite simply they do not have adequate facilities in place to deal with the enormity of post-Brexit trade. Ports in the UK and Europe are not up to managing the high volume of freight, they lack the necessary infrastructure involved in clearing customs posts. The UK does not at present have the capacity to dramatically improve the UK's customs facilities to deal with trade coming from the remaining EU states. Planning for what would be a series of major construction projects has not yet begun, and nor have the financial resources been allocated. Serious question marks exist over France's ability, let alone willingness, to upgrade their facilities to deal with trade coming from the UK.

Furthermore, a special UK-EU agreement on customs clearance must be in place by Spring 2019. Without such an agreement, there will be trade gridlock. That is unless trade can be rerouted through the near century of British ports to the plethora of customs posts across the continent of Europe. Yet it is not just the physicality of the trade that needs to be addressed. The technical side will require the UK to develop and agree and put in place a computer system to facilitate the easy passage of goods. This must be compatible with systems in the remaining EU.

Tariffs in themselves are not the issue, time is. The cost of collecting the customs duties, a set percentage of their sale price agreed with the WTO and charged to the importer, makes any financial benefit for the EU almost irrelevant. Any 'benefit' comes from increasing a rival's costs to protect EU producers. However, with increasingly interdependent markets, with global value chains where the genesis of a manufacture rests in many nations which have supplied the numerous parts, such a strategy makes little economic sense.

The real advantage of eliminating tariffs for the exporter, and the business importing the product, is not the removal of this tax on trade. The main benefit is that, without the need to produce the paperwork and payments to meet these customs duties, the item will not be subject to delays.

Before solutions can be found to ease the process of trade, the hoops and obstacles need to be explored. All non-EU companies that send goods to the EU must either pay tariffs, complete paper work, and clear customs; sending the goods to be approved via a designated port of entry. Even if a free trade agreement is in place customs officers checking products and making sure the necessary bureaucracy is complete is still a legal requirement.

Concern five: There will be complex new 'rules of origin' and additional paperwork for British goods

Another area in which the EU could try to 'punish' the UK would be in the form of new red tape and potentially costly and complicated new 'rules of origin' (ROO) for British exporters.

If a business is sending produce to the EU from a country that has a free trade deal it must prove that they were mostly manufactured or re-worked in a country that has such an agreement with the EU. If the business cannot confirm the origin of the goods, then the tariffs will apply. This can be sidestepped by making some modifications to the products in the exporting state, yet this may be subject to investigation. This is an infrequent occurrence, yet the need for paperwork to prove its provenance is not rare.

If the goods are of UK origin and if Britain has a free trade agreement, namely no tariffs to pay, importing into an EU country will require a Certificate of Origin. Such documentation can be obtained from a relevant countries chamber of commerce, they are however expensive.

Anything that is already inside the customs union that has originated from a non-member will have been charged a tariff at its original port of entry and can therefore circulate freely within the EU. At present, as the UK is an integral part of the EU's customs union, British exporters to the other 27 do not have to prove that they comply with the EU's rules of origin. Goods entering the UK from outside the EU will have been charged the relevant customs duty when entering Britain. As supply chains are becoming increasingly globalised the need to demonstrate an item's origins can be a complex burden.

The Trade Policy Research Centre argued that 'the process of adapting to rules of origin based duty-free trade under a new UK-EU free trade agreement would be tedious, costly and disruptive to trade.'[35] However, some developments are making this concern less relevant. The reduction in tariffs, where many goods are zero rated, reduces the need to complete the administrative duties. The EU has extended the area in which origin can be accumulated to not only cover more states but also to allow for an item to be obtained and manufactured in a number of countries without the final product losing the benefit of being tariff free when it enters the EU. This system has been in existence in the EU and European Free Trade Association since 1997 and for Turkey since 1999. Over time the EU does grant greater allowance to other countries to claim exception from rules of origin. And from 2017 under World Customs Union rules the procedure declaring a products origin will be further simplified.

As WTO members, the UK and EU are signed up to the WTO agreement on Rules of Origin in which signatories 'Recognizing that it is desirable to provide transparency of laws, regulations, and practices regarding rules of origin' affirm that they are committed:

'…to ensure that rules of origin themselves do not create unnecessary obstacles to trade.

'Agree that:

'Members shall ensure that their rules of origin are not used as instruments to pursue trade objectives directly or indirectly; rules of origin shall not themselves create restrictive, distorting, or disruptive effects on international trade.

---

35   Ronald Stewart-Brown and Felix Bungay, *Rules of Origin in EU Free Trade Agreements, Trade Policy Research Centre*, 2012

'They shall not pose unduly strict requirements or require the fulfilment of a certain condition not related to manufacturing or processing, as a prerequisite for the determination of the country of origin.

'The rules of origin that they apply to imports and exports are not more stringent than the rules of origin they apply to determine whether or not a good is domestic and shall not discriminate between other Members, irrespective of the affiliation of the manufacturers of the good concerned.

'Their rules of origin are administered in a consistent, uniform, impartial and reasonable manner.'

Rules of origin disputes in the WTO system are overseen by the WTO Committee on Rules of Origin and the WCO Technical Committee.[36]

The UK is also a member of the WCO (World Customs Organization) an international body which works closely with the WTO and WCO member countries to identify, minimise and resolve problems such as rules of origin and other customs issues.

WORLD CUSTOMS ORGANIZATION

The EU is also a member of the WCO, as are its member states.

The European Commission website confirms that:

'On 30 June 2007, the Council of the World Customs Organization (WCO) decided to accept the request of the European Union to join the WCO as of 1st July 2007. This decision grants to the European Union rights and obligations on an interim basis akin to those enjoyed by WCO Members. The EU is a contracting party to several WCO Conventions, and contributes to the work of this organisation.'[37]

The EU cannot therefore; arbitrarily impose red tape or inordinate Rules of Origin requirements upon the UK and still meet its WCO obligations.

The EU is also signed up to the GATT agreement which states that:

'The contracting parties also recognize the need for minimizing the incidence and complexity of import and export formalities and for decreasing and simplifying import and export documentation requirements.

'No contracting party shall impose substantial penalties for minor breaches of customs regulations or procedural requirements. In particular, no penalty in respect of any omission or mistake in customs

---

36   https://www.wto.org/english/tratop_e/roi_e/roi_info_e.htm

37   https://ec.europa.eu/taxation_customs/business/international-affairs/international-customs-cooperation-mutual-administrative-assistance-agreements/world-customs-organization_en

documentation which is easily rectifiable and obviously made without fraudulent intent or gross negligence shall be greater than necessary to serve merely as a warning.'[38]

When we combine all these points with the fact that the EU and its member states are also signed up to the WTO agreement on trade facilitation, the potential risks of additional red tape and paperwork for importers and exporters look less and less likely, post Brexit.

Even if the EU wished to try to impose trading barriers in this way, there would be a substantive knock-on effect to the EU-UK cross border supply chains as a consequence. They will be aware of this, and all sides will wish to minimize this possibility from occurring by ensuring ROO requirements and other forms of red tape are kept to a minimum.

Finally, imposing difficult new ROO procedures upon the UK would be going against the EU's 'direction of travel' in this area, which is to simplify and relax their rules (with a special focus on simplifying them for developing countries).[39] In 2010, the European Commission admitted that:

'The present rules of origin are old and outdated, having been drawn up in the 1970s. The commercial world has changed with globalisation, and the rules have long been criticised as being both too complex and too stringent.

'The European Commission adopted a communication in 2005 which argued that the rules needed to be made simpler…this communication was based on three pillars: appropriate rules for the determination of origin; efficient procedures; and a secured environment for legitimate trade."[40]

The new rules will be implemented by the EU in 2017.

---

38   https://www.wto.org/english/docs_e/legal_e/gatt47_e.pdf

39   https://ec.europa.eu/taxation_customs/business/calculation-customs-duties/rules-origin/general-aspects-preferential-origin/new-developments_en

40   http://europa.eu/rapid/press-release_MEMO-10-588_en.htm?locale=en

Concern six: UK businesses will face barriers from accessing EU financial markets

One concern which may have some real legitimacy is the possibility that UK businesses will face barriers from accessing EU financial markets. Of particular concern is the potential loss of 'passporting' rights.

These are defined by The Financial Conduct Authority (FCA) as carrying out cross-border trade in services by either establishing a subsidiary in another jurisdiction and trading through that entity, this is called 'branch passporting'. The alternative, known as 'services passporting' is conducting this trade across borders.[41]

The ability of British based financial institutions to trade with countries, businesses and individuals on the continent is a great benefit to the UK economy. At the same time, Britain is being held back by the EU's reticence at making trade agreements, an exclusive EU competence, with emerging markets around the world that include access to services markets. EU membership has meant that Britain could not make agreements that allowed our great strength, the services industry, to fully engage with other markets around the world. Instead of looking at the enormous opportunities that Brexit presents, the debate so far has focused on the risks of losing access to the EU's single market.

Prior to the Brexit referendum, the government sought to claim that the EU's services market could be of particular benefit to the British economy. The government argued that if the EU completes the single market in services – opening-up all member states to competition – the UK's economic output could be boosted by as much as 7%.[42] The completion of the single market in services always was a very big if. Indeed, it is illusory. Many EU states have still have not properly implemented the EU's services directive and are unlikely to do so. Keeping in place restrictive practices and barriers to entry against foreign (British) competition.

That said, the services industry is still an especially important part of the UK's economic links with the EU. In 2011 the UK's trade in goods with the EU was in deficit by around £43 billion; however, trade in services was in surplus by £16 billion. This reduced the overall deficit to approximately £28 billion.[43]

The UK's entire financial services sector supports the resulting and even larger international business services industry. Research published by the Bruges Group found that 'in the fourth quarter of 2013 business services accounted for 1,517,000 jobs in London, which was 28% of all London employment. (Their proportion of UK employment as a whole was 15.7%.)

> 'These businesses are based primarily in or around the capital. London-based international business services (i.e., both financial and non- financial services) employ about 5% of the UK's working population and produce perhaps 8% - 10% of its national output, with most of that output exported. Continued growth of these activities at above the growth rate of output as a whole would be positive for the UK's average living standards.'

---

41   https://www.fca.org.uk/firms/passporting

42   Department for Business Innovation and Skills, BIS Economics Paper No. 11, The economic consequences for the UK and the EU of completing the Single Market, February 2011, page vi

http://www.bis.gov.uk/assets/BISCore/economics-and-statistics/
     docs/E/11-517-economic-consequences-of-completing-single-market.pdf

43   http://www.theyworkforyou.com/lords/?id=2012-11-14a.1507.0

Of all the concerns outlined in this report, loss of financial services access represents the biggest threat to the UK economy, as much of our economy is geared towards the services industry.

However, these problems are not insurmountable.

There is the example of the Swiss, like Britain they have a strong financial services industry. Although they have a series of bi-lateral free trade agreements with the EU in goods these do not cover the export of services.

Swiss-based companies do not have the right to sell their services to the EU unless they establish a subsidiary inside the European Economic Area. This is not an insurmountable problem. Multi-national companies, by definition, can and do establish themselves in different jurisdictions. However, small and medium-sized enterprises will find creating subsidiaries burdensome. Restricting opportunities to tap into the EU's internal market. Better alternatives do exist.

The Swiss experience is that rules that would deprive British financial service firms from operating inside the remaining EEA can be sidestepped. A Swiss report found that *'Though extremely cumbersome this does give them full access to the EU market.'*[44] However, if the subsidiaries are based in the EU they will be subject to the same heavy handed bureaucracies which have the power to close a financial institution operating inside the European Union. These are: -

- The EBA (European Banking Authority)
- European Insurance and Occupational Pensions Authority
- European Systemic Risk Board
- European Securities and Markets Authority (ESMA)
- Community Programme for Financial Reporting and Auditing

The benefits of Brexit need to be reiterated. The City of London will be free from EU debt risks and its businesses will not be subject to European Union tax, an area which the EU is steadily expanding into, in particular the Common Consolidated Corporate Tax Base (CCCTB). The City of London will also be free from an EU Financial Transaction Tax. Britain will also be able to disregard the regulations that threaten pay within the financial services sector, such as; 'Recommendation on remuneration the financial sector 32009H0384'.

There is however a new hope. This is driven by mutual self-interest.

According to Mark Carney, the Governor of the Bank of England;

> *"Banks located in the UK supply over half of debt and equity issuance by continental firms, and account for over three-quarters of foreign exchange and derivatives activity in the EU."*[45]

Quite clearly, businesses in the EU need the City of London. However, despite this powerful incentive for the EU to keep in place Britain's passporting rights there are still procedures that must be followed. It could be granted through the withdrawal agreement that would in theory emerge from the Article 50 negotiations. That is presuming that any agreement does not become regarded as one that needs the approval of all EU member states Parliaments, as an Association Agreement would so require.

---

44   Centre for Swiss Politics, University of Kent, *Switzerland's Approach to EU Engagement: A Financial Services Perspective*, City of London, April 2013, page 4

45   http://www.telegraph.co.uk/business/2016/11/30/mark-carney-warns-eu-faces-financial-drought-cuts-uk-overnight/

There are still ways to resolve this issue. If the UK follows the same general regulatory framework as businesses in the EU, then the European regulators can grant what is known as 'equivalence'. This should not be too difficult for the UK. Presently, Britain follows the same regulations as the rest of the EU. What is more, according to a report by the House of Lords the UK would have implemented 41 of 42 EU financial services regulations even if Britain was not an EU member. The exception was the Alternative Investment Fund Managers Directive (AIFMD). This is not surprising, the genesis of many of these rules is from global bodies. For instance, the WTO, OECD, IMF, the Bank of International Settlements, and the Financial Stability Board. Indeed, Mark Carney is the Chairman of this body and guides the development if its proposals. Through his international role, the Governor of the Bank of England, has been developing global rules on financial services, putting Britain firmly at the top table. It should also be noted that equivalence is not the same as harmonisation. The UK does not need to have identical financial services regulation to the EU. To qualify for equivalence, the regulatory framework just needs to be compatible and comparable.

Furthermore, the proposed Great Repeal Bill, as proposed by Prime Minister Theresa May, will incorporate into British law all existing EU legislation. Thus continuing the rules upon which the industry operates after Brexit as before, keeping the UK, at least for the medium term, fully qualified to achieve access to the EU based on equivalence.

The EU rules that can grant financial firms based in the UK access derive from most of the financial services legislation itself. For example Article 46(1) of The Markets in Financial Instruments (MiFIR). It grants non-EEA based firms the right to provide investment services in the single market without the need to establish a subsidiary in the EEA and without the provider being under the control of an EU member states national regulator.

To have this access, according to DLA Piper, there are a number of requirements:

(i) the firm is authorised in its home country and subject to supervision and enforcement by the relevant regulator (eg by the Financial Conduct Authority)

(ii) a positive equivalence determination from the European Securities and Markets Authority (ESMA) that the legal and supervisory arrangement of the third country have equivalent effect to the prudential and business conduct requirements under MiFID II

(iii) cooperation arrangements between ESMA and the third country authority specifying the exchange of information mechanism, the prompting notification for breaches and the coordination of supervisory activities, and...

(iv) registration with ESMA (which is dependent on the above having occurred).[46]

Access for non-EEA alternative investment fund managers is also granted by Article 35, 39 to 41 of the AIFM directive; as long as they are operating under an equivalent jurisdiction. This again is subject to determination by the ESMA.

In other areas of financial activity, selling financial services across a border into the EU is provided for by EU laws such as; the Capital Requirements Directive, UCITS Directive, Insurance Distribution Directive, Electronic Money Directive, Solvency II Directive, Payment Services Directive and the Mortgage Credit Directive.[47]

---

46   https://www.dlapiper.com/en/uk/insights/publications/2016/07/no-more-passporting-post-brexit/

47   http://www.bankofengland.co.uk/pra/Pages/authorisations/passporting/default.aspx

The EU has also signed several agreements with third countries that contain trade in services provisions, so precedents do exist.

The Rt Hon. Peter Lilley, writing for the Conservative Home website has suggested that the loss of automatic EU passporting rights might not be such a huge loss to the UK.

'The value of passporting rights, though worth keeping, should not be exaggerated. I say that as the Minister who negotiated the first passporting directive and later implemented the Single Market programme.

'UK-based financial services firms have passporting rights as a member of the EU.

'But so too under The Markets in Financial Instruments Directive (MIFID2) Directive financial services companies from countries such as the US, Hong Kong and Singapore, whose financial regulatory systems are deemed to have 'regulatory equivalence', as would the UK's.'[48]

Former Shadow Chief Secretary to the Treasury Lord Howard Flight, writing for the same website explained why it would be mutually beneficial for both the UK and EU to come to an agreement in this area:

'There is also the important issue of branches versus subsidiaries. Most of the large London institutions already have branches or subsidiaries within the EU and even more EU organisations have branches in London. If EU entities were required to establish subsidiaries in the UK, this would be extremely costly. There are over 70 EU banks in London under branch "passports" and thus not under Prudential Regulation Authority regulation.

'The MiFID II Equivalence Passporting will include investment banks and should, therefore, enable branch operations to continue both ways. Equivalence Passporting arrangements will need to be registered with the EU Securities and Market Authority (ESMA). Already Australia, Bermuda, Hong Kong, Mexico, Singapore and the US have achieved deemed Equivalence for reinsurance services.

'Moodys have already argued that the City can cope reasonably without Single Market Passporting, rather using Equivalence Passporting.'[49]

This route may however prove to be a lengthy process, requiring registration and there is no guarantee that the politics of Europe will be easily obliging to a post-Brexit Britain.

There is however another way that the City's interests can be protected. The World Trade Organisation, through building upon the General Agreement on Trade in Services,[50] is seeking to create international agreements that will dramatically open-up access to markets in services.[51] [52] What is more, the EU is fully engaged with these negotiations. In time, an independent UK should be able to take advantage of WTO proposals for a streamlined "single window" through which businesses can trade their services across national boundaries.

---

48   http://www.conservativehome.com/platform/2016/09/peter-lilley-brexit-should-be-swift-heres-how-to-do-it.html

49   http://www.conservativehome.com/thecolumnists/2016/10/howard-flight-negotiating-a-brexit-passport-to-success-for-the-city-of-london.html

50   https://www.wto.org/english/docs_e/legal_e/26-gats_01_e.htm

51   https://www.wto.org/english/news_e/news16_e/serv_05oct16_e.htm

52   https://www.wto.org/english/news_e/news16_e/snegs_14nov16_e.htm

While the EU, its member states and the UK are all signatories to the WTO General Agreement on Trade in Services (GATS), this agreement on its own does not in itself guarantee that UK firms access to sell their services (financial or other) into the EU or vice-versa.

As the researcher Ben Clements wrote in his IEA Brexit prize submission:

'…the degree to which market access can be facilitated would often be considerably more limited for UK exporters under the GATS arrangement compared with the current arrangement for numerous reasons.

'Barriers to services frequently arise through non-tariff barriers, for instance domestic laws and regulations. On the whole, services markets are regulated to a greater extent compared with the market for goods.

'Member states of the EU maintain a great deal of discretion concerning services regulation and administration.'[53]

The City of London brings capital to this country financing wealth creation as well as pubic services throughout the land. It attracts skills and other businesses supporting the wider British economy. Yet, the EU restricts the opportunities open to the City. At the same time, leaving does present challenges. The solutions, however, just like the opportunities, are global.

The UK's financial services industry has a global role and should not be hemmed into little declining Europe. The City of London should not be afraid to make the switch. Not only do great prospects await it, there is the real likelihood that Britain's financial services industry will, through the many routes open to it, be able to keep its access to the EU's single market whilst also not remaining a part of the internal market.

One final point on services – the EU is currently negotiating an international agreement on services including financial services, called the Trade in Services Agreement (TiSA).

'The 21st TiSA negotiating round took place from 2 to 10 November 2016 and was organised and chaired by the EU. The talks are progressing well.[54]

'Parties made good progress in working towards an agreed text"[55]

It could be the case therefore that even if the UK was unable to sign a specific UK-EU agreement regarding services after Brexit, the UK could take part in the TiSA agreement when that is concluded.

Whether via equivalence agreements, the TiSA or something similar or UK banks using brass plate subsidiaries in the EEA, the UK financial services sector would eventually find some way to carry on, making it business as usual.

Yet in order to guarantee this, we believe the UK negotiating team should make a deal on financial services top on their list of negotiating priorities, although (according to rumour) it already has.

53   https://iea.org.uk/wp-content/uploads/2016/07/Clement%20BREXIT%20entry_for%20web_0.pdf

54   http://ec.europa.eu/trade/policy/in-focus/tisa/index_en.htm

55   http://trade.ec.europa.eu/doclib/docs/2016/november/tradoc_155095.pdf

Concern seven: The EU will try to stop the UK accessing EU-third country trade deals

The Secretary of State for International Trade (and President of the Board of Trade) Dr Liam Fox MP told the House of Commons[56] on 3rd November 2016:

"The EU has some 36 free trade agreements, which cover more than 50 countries.

"A very large number of those have already made representations to the United Kingdom to say that they would like those agreements to continue[57]. We will explore and discuss that, because, as I have said, our aim is to have no break in access to markets and to achieve the transition as smoothly as possible, with minimal disruption to the international trading environment."

The Lawyers for Britain[58] group has reported that it may be quite simple for the UK to retain access to these trade deals:

'The EU has existing free trade agreements which currently apply to the UK as an EU member. Most of these EU agreements are with micro-States or developing countries and only a small number represent significant export markets for the UK. Both the EU and the member states (including the UK) are parties to these agreements.

'The UK could simply continue to apply the substantive terms of these agreements on a reciprocal basis after exit unless the counterparty State were actively to object. We can see no rational reason why the counterparty States would object to this course since that would subject their existing export trade into the UK market, which is currently tariff free, to new tariffs. There will be no need for complicated renegotiation of these existing agreements as was misleadingly claimed by pro-Remain propaganda.'

They go on to conclude that:

'…this kind of "rolling over" of treaty obligations is a familiar process in international law. It happens in cases of "State succession" where an existing State splits and the component parts wish to continue existing treaty relationships with other States. For example, when Czechoslovakia split into the separate states of the Czech Republic and Slovakia on 31 December 1992, both new States agreed to assume and continue to honour the treaty obligations of the former State of Czechoslovakia, and other States and international bodies accepted the succession as being effective, where necessary agreeing new machinery for the separate representation of the two new States.

'The exit of the UK from the EU is not legally a case of State succession. As explained above, the UK will reassume the full powers of its existing Statehood by re-assuming rights and responsibilities for its own international relations in areas at present where its interests are represented via the EU. However, the practical issues involved are very similar and there is a similar mutual interest in preserving the continuity of existing treaty arrangements, particularly those which affect day-to-day existing trade, unless there is some good and concrete reason for changing those arrangements. It follows that the international counterparties to the existing EU FTAs will almost certainly follow

---

56   https://hansard.parliament.uk/commons/2016-11-03/debates/4D25DC63-B095-4C8F-B027-A4363A067A0C/
      TopicalQuestions

57   http://www.thetimes.co.uk/edition/news/trading-partners-want-to-keep-eu-deal-terms-after-brexit-says-fox-v3zdzbndw

58   http://www.lawyersforbritain.org/index.shtml

general State practice in State succession cases and accept the rolling over of FTA arrangements so that they continue to apply to the UK after Brexit.'

EU Researcher Dr Richard North concurs with this analysis, writing that:

'…third country treaties are manageable. For the most part, ensuring continuance is a relatively minor administrative task that can be resolved relatively simply.

'The [Vienna] Convention sets out the procedures for carrying over treaties, where all parties agree to their continuation. It allows for the newly independent State – in this case the UK – to establish its status as a party to an existing treaty by way of a formal notification of succession, lodged with the depository of each treaty.

'There is no question of any need for major renegotiations. Even if a few have to be renegotiated, that is not necessarily a significant problem. Talks may be relatively trouble-free and speedy to conclude.'[59]

Whilst the EU does have exclusive power over the negotiation of trade agreements, those deals are mostly mixed agreements and the member states are parties to them as well as the EU. To come into force they must have had to be signed by the member states in order for them to be ratified.[60] Most of the trade agreements in place have been put into domestic law and bind each country.

All that is needed is for the parties to the treaties to agree to their continuing. This is straightforward and set out in Article 38 of the Vienna Convention. Furthermore, the 1978 Vienna Convention on the Succession of States in respect of Treaties may also have relevance.

Article 34 on Succession of States in cases of separation of parts of a State reads;

'1.When a part or parts of the territory of a State separate to form one or more States, whether or not the predecessor State continues to exist:

(a) any treaty in force at the date of the succession of States in respect of the entire territory of the predecessor State continues in force in respect of each successor State so formed…'

Suggesting that trade deals that the EU has signed on its members behalf, or as itself, will continue after we leave and apply to the departing state.

The very worst case scenario is that the parties, UK and the country to which the third country just need to deposit notification, with the UN, or just inform the other parties if it's not deposited at the UN, that the treaties will continue and apply to UK after our secession. In other words, all these trade treaties don't need to be renegotiated by an independent UK. Trade with other nations around the globe will continue as before.

With the right negotiations then, accessing EU-third country trade deals might not be the daunting and mammoth task that some commentators seem to think. It will be in all countries interests for things to continue with as little disruption as possible after Brexit.

59   http://www.eureferendum.com/blogview.aspx?blogno=85960

60   http://eur-lex.europa.eu/legal-content/EN/TXT/?uri=URISERV%3Aai0034

Concern eight – The EU will demand access to our fishing waters

Does Brexit mean Brexit, with the change that we need, or will it just be business as usual?

The EU's Common Fisheries Policy is a drain on the British economy. A condition of entry into the EEC, as it was then, the British Government was required to surrender control over its fishing waters on 1st January 1973. When, Britain's chief negotiator with the EEC, Sir Con O'Neill, was discussing the UK's terms of entry he was shocked at the fishing demands. He warned Edward Heath, but the then PM betrayed the industry and told him to "swallow the lot and swallow it now". Under United Nations rules a country now has the right, even the responsibility, to control the sea around its coast stretching out for a total of 200 miles or until the median line between two adjacent nations.

The European Commission opened UK waters to all other member states fishing fleets, apportioning fishing rights as they see fit. The Common Fisheries Policy costs Britain more than £3.7 billion per year caused through the EU depriving the UK of its valuable fishing grounds.

In 2012 UK fishing vessels landed 627,000 tonnes of sea fish (including shellfish) this yearly catch has a value of £770 million.[61] This is 13% of the value for the total EU catch.[62] In 2012 British vessels account for approximately 12% - 13% of the total size of the EU catch.[63] This figure remains relatively constant. In 2010 the total EU catch amounted to 4,923,000 tonnes, the share of this going to UK fishermen is 608,000 tonnes.[64] The British catch in 2010 was again approximately 12% - 13% of the total for the EU.

This means that the EU fishing industry is worth £6.4 billion. Approximately 70% of this catch is taken in what were once British fishing waters, now governed by the EU and open to vessels from other EU member states. This means that if these waters were fully reserved for UK fishermen, which would be legal under international law, then British fishing vessels would be able to land nearly £4.5 billion worth of fish. Yet the clear majority is being lost to our competitors in the EU, with British fisherman only being able to land £770,000 worth of fish.

Other estimates suggest that 80% of the total EU catch comes from what are, by United Nations standards, British waters. This would put the figure of the total resource taken from UK control by the EU at more than £5 billion.

The problems of the CFP are not just economic. The EU's quota restrictions have had a disastrous environmental impact. For decades, if a vessel landed more than its allotted amount they must then discard the fish that exceed the legal limit set by EU policy. The result was that as much as two thirds were returned to sea dead. Subsequently fish stocks declined significantly; further reducing the bounty of the sea. This policy has turned the once abundant North Sea into an ecological crisis zone. After more than four decades there has finally been some change, but the discard ban will only address the symptom of the EU's disastrous free for all policy, the discarding of fish, rather than the actual cause,

61   http://www.marinemanagement.org.uk/fisheries/statistics/documents/ukseafish/2012/final.pdf

62   The European Fishing Industry, Struan Stevenson MEP, President of the Fisheries Committee of the European Parliament, page 9 http://epp.eurostat.ec.europa.eu/statistics_explained/index.php?title=File:Total_catches_in_all_fishing_ regions,_2000-2010_(1_000_tonnes_live_weight).png&filetimestamp=20121022153701

63   http://www.europarl.europa.eu/aboutparliament/en/displayFtu.html?ftuId=FTU_5.3.9.html

64   http://epp.eurostat.ec.europa.eu/statistics_explained/index.php?title=File:Total_catches_in_all_fishing_regions,_2000-2010_(1_000_tonnes_live_weight).png&filetimestamp=20121022153701

the EU's control over quotas. The British fishing fleet was decimated by this as vessels must stop fishing when they exhaust their quota allocation.

The devastation on this industry can be measured by its human impact. In 1970 there were 21,443 fishermen in the UK; by 2012 that figure had been cut back to just 12,445.[65] The loss of jobs and the once active fishing fleet also had a detrimental effect on secondary industries that supported the fishing fleet and benefitted from the proceeds from this once sizeable business.[66]

The effect of EU control via the Common Fisheries Policy has been to seriously damage a once strong industry. Landings into the UK have fallen from 1,039,100 tonnes in 1970 to just 489,100 in 2012. This steady decline has led to a growing dependency upon imports. In 2010, a total of 687,054 tonnes of seafood worth £2.23 billion was imported into Britain.[67] That is British people having to buy back our own fish form foreign competitors. This must change, and with Brexit it should, but will it…?

This subsidising of foreign fleets by British consumers could be reduced if UK fishermen had their exclusive rights restored to them. There must be the full repatriation of UK resources and a fit for purpose UK policy implemented to allow the rejuvenation of this multi-billion-pound industry.

However, it is proposed by the Prime Minister Theresa May to incorporate the entire body of EU law, known as the *Acquis Communautaire*, into UK law. This will be via the so-called Great Repeal Bill. Yet, all EU law will include the legislation that underpins the Common Fisheries Policy (CFP).

The CFP is a reprehensible policy, both in terms of conservation and in operation. It would be expedient and advisable diplomatically and politically, that no facet of it is replicated, transposed or continued into UK law. Doing so would be to risk recognising in UK law the mechanisms of the EU's policy – especially EU "equal access" and resources shares. That would be an abject betrayal of Brexit.

The CFP is constructed entirely of Regulations (direct EU law). Under the terms of Article 50, section 3, "the treaties shall cease to apply", consequently so will the regulations and therefore the entire CFP and all mechanisms of it. The UK would revert to full control of our waters and all resources therein under international law (UNCLOS 3), with a clean slate to implement our own policy like Norway, Iceland and the Faroe Islands successfully manage.

Foreign fleets do not have the right to exploit the UK's Exclusive Economic Zone (EEZ) regime, which is from 12 miles up to 200 miles, or the median line from Britain's shores to that of another state. By accepting this policy other EU, coastal States have given up any claims they may have had, with regard to fishing in what will become the UK's EEZ, based on traditional or historic fishing rights. Second, although historic/traditional fishing rights may still exist alongside the EEZ regime, such rights are subject to recognition by the coastal state in whose EEZ the rights are being exercised. Finally, historic fishing rights may play a role in the delimitation of overlapping EEZs, but only in exceptional circumstances.[68] So it seems that, as suggested, the interlopers will not be able to keep fishing without the UK's approval (as long as we do not keep the CFP regime when Brexit takes place). Perhaps the European Union will reimburse the fishing industry in Morocco which bought the right to fish in what should be the UK's Exclusive Economic Zone.

65   UK Sea Fisheries Statistics 2007, Marine & Fisheries Agency, 2012, page 24 http://www.marinemanagement.org.uk/fisheries/statistics/documents/ukseafish/2012/final.pdf

66   Batten, Gerard, *How Much Does the European Union Cost Britain?* 2008, the Bruges Group

67   http://www.seafish.org/media/486918/faqs%20web%20version%20010711.pdf

68   https://www.law.berkeley.edu/files/Bernard-final.pdf

The proposed Great Repeal Bill, as it stands, however, would negate this by adopting the CFP onto the UK statute book. This may prevent us from rebuilding and rejuvenating the industry and our long suffering coastal communities. If Parliament passes a bill that adopts into UK law the Common Fisheries Policy, along with all its iniquities, then our Members of Parliament will be betraying the industry again, just as they did in 1972 when the European Communities Act was passed into law.

To make sure that our fisheries are protected, the adoption of EU law into British law must exclude the Common Fisheries Policy. It is an area where UK law, and a sustainable policy for the benefit of our home fleet, should be put into place as soon as we leave the European Union. There must be no transition, it must be instantaneous.

Future policy must scrap all EU mechanisms, move to a Days-at-Sea, keep what you catch system, that is applicable to mixed fisheries – the Faroe Islands set this precedent in 1996.

The UK's fishing industry could be a triumph for Brexit and Britain. The fishing industry and the communities that depend upon it can be saved as long as the Government exempts fisheries from the Great Repeal Bill, and puts into place our own policy. Indeed, British fishing can thrive as a world leader alongside other independent nations who fish the North Sea; Norway, Iceland and the Faroe Islands.

The British fishing industry was betrayed and bartered as expendable by Edward Heath when he sought to join the EEC. Fishing has become a microcosm and epitomises both the disaster of EU interference and incompetency. Due to this, fishing will be symbolic of withdrawal and will be the acid test of whether Brexit means Brexit, with the change that we need.

Fishing could be held up as a beacon of the Government's resolve and whether they can make a success of Brexit. As a nation, we should be bold. Aside from the London Convention of 1964, which granted rights to those who had habitually fished between the 6 and 12-mile limit for the 10 years prior to 1964, there is no provision for historic rights under international law on fisheries for the fishing limits from 12 to the 200-mile limit. It is the 200-mile limit that was snatched by the EEC as the price for admission into what became the EU. All current 'rights' for other EU fleets, and anyone else the European Commission has sold access to fish in our waters, comes via EU law. We can take back control from those interlopers, unless we are foolish enough to put those same regulations into force ourselves.

We need a British fishing policy ready to replace the failed EU system. Post-Brexit fishing policy should be managed by the UK on a regional basis. With responsibility for implementation and enforcement being passed, where relevant to the devolved institutions in Scotland, Wales and Northern Ireland. Who should then follow a days at sea regime rather than quotas. And have a firm ban on the discarding of fish. Discarding was the ravenous policy of returning caught, and usually expired, fish back to the deep when a quota was exceeded and a more profitable catch was detected. Outside the EU Britain should look to develop fishing policy alongside the Codex Committee on Fish and Fishery Products (CCFFP) based in Norway.

Concern nine: Security co-operation and cross-border Crime prevention

Amber Rudd, the Home Secretary has said that: "Europol has played an important role in keeping us safe and we will be having discussions about how to continue some form of involvement within the agencies of the EU that help to keep us safe."[69]

This does not necessarily mean however; that the UK should seek to continue as a full member of EUROPOL. Several non-EU countries have signed Operational Agreements or Strategic Agreements with EUROPOL and so the UK could likely do the same. Examples include the USA, Norway and Canada.[70]

The EU is in fact obligated to work with the UK on Transnational Organized Crime as it is a signatory to the United Nations Convention Against Transnational Organized Crime (agreed in 2000).[71]

[Interestingly, under Article 103 of the UN charter, in the event of a conflict between the obligations of the Members of the United Nations under the Charter (and by implication, UN Conventions and protocols) and their obligations under any other international agreement, their obligations under the UN take greater precedence.]

International Criminal Court

INTERPOL

UNODC
United Nations Office on Drugs and Crime

World Customs Organization
Organisation Mondiale des Douanes

Additional cross-border crime prevention efforts can be conducted via the International Criminal Police Organisation INTERPOL, the Organization for Security and Co-operation in Europe (OSCE) the United Nations Office on Drugs and Crime (UNODC) and the World Customs Organisation (WCO).

Aside from the already mentioned organisations, work can continue via the 'Committee of Experts on the Operation of European Conventions on Co-operation in Criminal Matters (PC-OC)' which works under the Council of Europe Framework. To quote their website:

'The Council of Europe's Committee of Experts on the Operation of European Conventions on Co-operation in Criminal Matters (PC-OC / Terms of reference) is the forum in which, since 1981, experts from all member and observer states and organisations come together to

69 http://www.express.co.uk/news/uk/709745/What-is-Europol-Will-UK-sign-up-EU-police-after-Brexit-european-union-leave

70 https://www.europol.europa.eu/partners-agreements

71 http://www.unodc.org/unodc/en/treaties/CTOC/index.html

elaborate ways to improve international co-operation in criminal matters and identify solutions to practical problems.'[72]

And of course, the UK would still work with the International Criminal Court (ICC).

Extradition

The UK should not seek to retain access to participation in the European Arrest Warrant (EAW). While arguments can be made for its retention, on balance it is flawed and continues to be a threat to civil liberties. It should be replaced by a new UK-EU agreement. The EU has the legal competence to negotiate such a treaty with a non-EU state; there is no need to re-negotiate with every EU member.

Leaving the EU does not mean that we will not be able to extradite or deport foreign criminals or bring criminals back to the UK to face punishment. Even without a new extradition treaty the previous arrangements between the UK and the individual EU member states will apply. Furthermore, the UK government website states:

> "Under multilateral conventions and bilateral extradition treaties the UK has extradition relations with over 100 territories around the world."[73]

Additionally, many EU and non-EU countries are signed up to the European Convention on Extradition[74].

72   http://www.coe.int/en/web/transnational-criminal-justice-pcoc/home_

73   https://www.gov.uk/guidance/extradition-processes-and-review

74   http://www.coe.int/en/web/conventions/full-list/-/conventions/rms/0900001680064587

Concern ten: Agriculture and EU protectionism and environmental matters

One of the most well-known and costly of Brussels' policies is the EU's system of agricultural support, payments and protection against competition from producers outside the EU, in particular developing nations. This is called the Common Agricultural Policy (CAP).

This policy makes up more than 40% of EU spending. In 2013 the EU spent €57.5 billion on subsidies to farmers and rural development. More than ten billion euros. The CAP as it is also known is a prime example of a policy that is not in the economic interests of British consumers. Whereas the UK only receives 7.6% of the European Agricultural Guarantee Fund, France receives 20%, the largest amount of any EU member state.[75]

According to written evidence provided by the charity Oxfam to the House of Commons Environmental Audit Committee, it is not just the British taxpayer that is losing out. Across the EU the CAP places €36.2 billion onto consumer's food bills. According to Oxfam, this costs a typical European family of four almost €1,000 a year in higher food prices.[76] That is €20 per week on the average family's food bill. This approximate figure is supported by the Paris based Organisation for Economic Co-operation and Development (OECD). This international organisation exists to promote trade and economic advancement. The OECD have estimated that the higher taxes and food prices caused through agricultural protectionism costs the family of four $1,000 per year. With food prices in the EU being as much as 30% higher than food which is traded internationally.

To whose benefit are these resources being spent? It is believed that the CAP's agricultural support payments are intended for small farmers however Oxfam make the case that 80% of the support goes to the wealthiest land owners and the largest agricultural businesses. The OECD also argue that in the European Union under the CAP system the richest 25% get 70% of the payments. And that 'Tens of thousands of small farm households benefit little from current farm policies.' And that 'of every $1 in price support, only $0.25 ends up in the farmer's pocket as extra income. The rest is absorbed by higher land prices, fertiliser and feed costs and other factors.'[77]

It is not just consumers that are losing out with British families paying a disproportionally high price for food imported from outside the European Union which must face EU customs taxes. Much of this is produced in developing nations and the Commonwealth; this prejudices trade with the farmers in those countries which also face quota restrictions. The CAP therefore has the notoriety for hurting both first world consumers and third world producers, whilst giving little benefit to small farmers.

There are other models of supporting farming from which the UK can learn. Payments, with a greater emphasis on supporting farmers in their role as custodians of the environment, needs to be enhanced with support directed away from the large landowners and agri-businesses to those that need it. The EU model of support, which is anti-consumer, is no longer sustainable.

What is more, Britain is a food importer, without an export market on the continent that is so significant that it would create ruin at home if it had to compete with the EU's protectionist agricultural policies. There

---

75   http://www.europarl.europa.eu/aboutparliament/en/displayFtu.html?ftuId=FTU_5.2.10.html

76   http://www.publications.parliament.uk/pa/cm201012/cmselect/cmenvaud/879/879vw27.htm

77   http://www.oecd.org/general/thedohadevelopmentroundoftradenegotiationsunderstandingtheissues.htm

are however still exports from the UK to the continent and some farmers may, unless the right policies are adopted, lose market share in the EU. The UK should use its political and economic influence, in particular our demand for foodstuffs from the continent, to make sure that exports from the UK are tariff free and not subject to restrictive quotas. Produce such as the trade in wheat and Meslin, which in 2010 amounted to over £460 million per year[78], should be high on the UK's agenda.

Leaving the EU will allow Britain to end inappropriate EU laws such as, stopping the transfer of whale product through UK ports such as Southampton.[79] Britain will also be able to end the export of live animals across the channel for slaughter.[80] The UK should then work through global bodies, such as the Codex Alimentarius Commission to set policy on food and its production.

Environmental matters

The nations of Europe can continue to co-operate on green issues after Brexit via the United Nations Environment Programme (UNEP) the Kyoto Protocol and the related United Nations Framework Convention on Climate Change (UNFCCC).

Additionally, the OSCE and UNECE both have environmental programmes we could continue to participate in, once we leave the EU.

---

78   https://www.statista.com/statistics/521078/wheat-and-meslin-export-value-united-kingdom-uk/

79   http://uk.whales.org/campaigns/help-stop-transfer-of-whale-products-through-eu-ports

80   http://www.hsa.org.uk/welfare-during-transport/welfare-during-transport

Conclusion

WTO Agreement on Trade Facilitation (TFA)[81]

Another nail in the coffin of the single market

Lord Lamont, the former UK Chancellor of the Exchequer wrote in *The Telegraph*:

'The single market is open to all advanced economies, in exchange for paying a relatively modest tariff of 3 to 4 per cent, something that evidently does not stop non-EU countries from selling within it.

'Every developed country has access to the single market. The EU has a relatively low external tariff with the exception of certain goods such as agriculture.'[82]

When taken *prima facie*, Lord Lamont's comments are seemingly correct. Only those countries who are essentially rogue states or have violated international agreements don't have the ability to conduct trade with the EU, and the EU's external tariffs are fairly low.

But Tariffs are only half of the story.

The problem of tariffs could be easily addressed by the UK signing a goods Free Trade Agreement (FTA) with the EU. Given the high volume of UK- EU 27 trade, this is seemingly a given.

A basic FTA need not take long to complete. The EU's earlier iteration the European Economic Community (EEC) concluded basic FTAs in the early 1970s that took 6-7 months to agree, sign and come into force.

But the other half of the story relates to non-tariff barriers (NTBs), sometimes called "Non-Tariff Measures (NTMs)". These comprise everything else that can slow down trade or make it more expensive or complex.

The European Commission describes the single market as:

'...one territory without any internal borders or other regulatory obstacles to the free movement of goods and services. The Commission works to remove or reduce barriers to intra-EU trade and prevent the creation of new ones so enterprises can trade freely in the EU and beyond. It applies Treaty rules prohibiting quantitative restrictions on imports and exports (Articles 34 to 36 TFEU) and manages the notification procedures on technical regulations (2015/1535) and technical barriers to trade.'[83]

So the single market goes beyond tariff reduction, and encompasses far more than just a free trade agreement. This is why the 'remain' side in the EU referendum campaign were so concerned about the UK leaving the European Union's single market.

'Remainers' believe that after Brexit, even if the UK does get a Free Trade Agreement, our importers and exporters will be deluged with red tape, endless forms, checks and other barriers to entry as we will be operating outside the single market.

These are valid concerns, but we believe they are largely exaggerated – and here are the reasons why:

---

81   https://www.wto.org/english/tratop_e/tradfa_e/tradfa_e.htm

82   http://www.telegraph.co.uk/news/2016/06/13/not-only-can-britain-can-leave-the-eu-and-have-access-to-the-sin/

83   https://ec.europa.eu/growth/single-market_en

— The EU has signed up to the WCO

In July 2007[84], the EU signed up to the World Customs Organization (WCO) which works to enhance customs co-operation between signatory countries and works to simplify issues such as Rules of Origin (ROO).

From the European Commission's own press release:

'On 30 June 2007, the Council of the World Customs Organization (WCO) decided to accept the request of the European Union to join the WCO as of 1st July 2007. This decision grants to the European Union *rights and obligations* on an interim basis akin to those enjoyed by WCO Members.

'The WCO plays an important role in promoting international customs co-operation and addressing new challenges for customs and trade. It is deeply involved in designing and implementing policies worldwide that integrate measures, which help ensure supply chain security, combat counterfeiting, promote trade and development, as well as guarantee efficient collection of customs revenues. Membership of the WCO highlights and confirms the central role and competence of the EU in international discussions on customs issues including customs reform. EU involvement in the WCO will focus on the full spectrum of customs issues, in particular the following broad areas:

- Nomenclature and classification in the framework of the Harmonised system;
- Origin of goods;
- Customs value;
- Simplification and harmonisation of customs procedures and trade facilitation;
- Development of supply chain security standards;
- Development of IPR enforcement standards;
- Capacity building for customs modernisation and reforms, including in the context of development cooperation;
- Mutual Administrative Assistance for the prevention, investigation and repression of customs offences.

'The EU is a contracting party to several WCO Conventions, and contributes to the work of this organisation, including by ensuring presence and coordination with the Member States in defining and representing EU positions in the relevant bodies managing these conventions.'

The UK signed up to the WCO in the 1950s and is a signatory in its own right, so will be able to address customs issues with the EU via this body after Brexit.

— Harmonisation with EU rules

The UK's rules and regulations are already synchronised with EU/EEA (European Economic Area) regulations and standards after decades of membership. This will also be true on the day after Brexit due to the Great Repeal Bill. Hence a strong (if not overwhelming) argument for 'rules equivalence' can be made.

---

84 https://ec.europa.eu/taxation_customs/business/international-affairs/international-customs-cooperation-mutual-administrative-assistance-agreements/world-customs-organization_en

— The WTO Agreement on Rules of Origin (ROO)

This agreement encourages WTO countries (including all EU countries) to have fair and transparent rules pertaining to Rules of Origin:

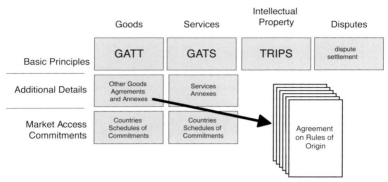

These rules state that:

> 'Rules of origin shall not themselves create restrictive, distorting, or disruptive effects on international trade. They shall not pose unduly strict requirements or require the fulfilment of a certain condition not related to manufacturing or processing, as a prerequisite for the determination of the country of origin....rules of origin are administered in a consistent, uniform, impartial and reasonable manner'.[85]

— Guidelines in the EU treaties

Article 8 of the Lisbon Treaty states that:

'The Union shall develop a special relationship with neighbouring countries, aiming to establish an area of prosperity and good neighbourliness, founded on the values of the Union and characterised by close and peaceful relations based on cooperation.'[86]

As the UK will become a new 'neighbouring country' after Brexit, the EU is compelled to deal with us according to the Article 8 terms.

— WTO Technical barriers to trade Agreement

The TBT agreement is key – it means that signatories (again, including the EU) agree to abide by rules about international product and technical standards. From the European Commission's website:

'The TBT notification procedure helps prevent the creation of international technical barriers to trade. It was introduced by the Agreement on Technical Barriers to Trade (the TBT Agreement), a multilateral agreement administered by the World Trade Organisation (WTO). It gives participants advanced knowledge of new technical regulations or conformity assessment procedures envisioned by other

---

85   https://www.wto.org/english/docs_e/legal_e/22-roo_e.htm

86   http://www.lisbon-treaty.org/wcm/the-lisbon-treaty/treaty-on-european-union-and-comments/title-1-common-provisions/6-article-8.html

countries. The EU's participation in the TBT Agreement helps businesses in EU countries access markets outside the EU.'

— Aim of the TBT notification procedure

To avoid any potential technical barriers to trade, WTO Members submit national legislation at draft stage to other members of the TBT Agreement. They can then assess the impact on their exports and identify any provisions breaching the Agreement.

While allowing all WTO Members to maintain their right to adopt regulations, the TBT Agreement aims to:

- prevent the creation of unnecessary and unjustified technical barriers to international trade;
- prevent the adoption of protectionist measures;
- encourage global harmonisation and mutual recognition of technical standards;
- Enhance transparency.[87]

The European Commission somewhat downplays the TBT agreement, however. What it actually states is that:

'Members shall ensure that in respect of technical regulations, products imported from the territory of any Member shall be accorded treatment no less favourable than that accorded to like products of national origin and to like products originating in any other country.

'Members shall ensure that technical regulations are not prepared, adopted or applied with a view to or with the effect of creating unnecessary obstacles to international trade.

'Where technical regulations are required and relevant international standards exist or their completion is imminent, Members shall use them, or the relevant parts of them, as a basis for their technical regulations. Members shall give positive consideration to accepting as equivalent technical regulations of other Members, even if these regulations differ from their own, provided they are satisfied that these regulations adequately fulfil the objectives of their own regulations.'[88]

Since UK regulations and standards will be equivalent to their EU counterparts from day one, and will continue to meet international standards going forward, it will be extremely difficult for the EU to reject UK products sold into the EU market.

— WTO Trade Facilitation Agreement

The most recent agreement, the WTO Trade Facilitation Agreement (TFA) will further increase trade co-operation.

As the WTO website states:

'The TFA contains provisions for expediting the movement, release and clearance of goods, including goods in transit. It also sets out measures for effective cooperation between customs and

---

87 https://ec.europa.eu/growth/single-market/barriers-to-trade/tbt_en

88 https://www.wto.org/english/docs_e/legal_e/17-tbt.pdf

other appropriate authorities on trade facilitation and customs compliance issues. It further contains provisions for technical assistance and capacity building in this area.'[89]

Perhaps especially important for Northern Ireland post-Brexit, the TFA also states that:

'Each Member shall ensure that its authorities and agencies responsible for border controls and procedures dealing with the importation, exportation, and transit of goods cooperate with one another and coordinate their activities in order to facilitate trade.

'Each Member shall, to the extent possible and practicable, cooperate on mutually agreed terms with other Members with whom it shares a common border with a view to coordinating procedures at border crossings to facilitate cross-border trade.'

The WCO welcomed the ratification of the TFA agreement in their press release of 22 February 2017, in which they wrote:

'The World Customs Organization (WCO) congratulates the World Trade Organization (WTO) on the entry into force today of the WTO Trade Facilitation Agreement; an agreement that will expedite the movement, release and clearance of goods, including goods in transit, and which sets out measures for effective cooperation between Customs and other authorities, as well as provisions for technical assistance and capacity building in this area.

'The WCO takes this opportunity to highlight that it will continue to seek improvements throughout the global supply chain to obtain the highest levels of safety, security and integrity, which will enhance trade facilitation for compliant actors. This will ultimately have a positive effect on the relationship between all border agencies and the Private Sector.

'The entry into force of the Trade Facilitation Agreement (TFA) is an important milestone for the international trade and Customs community, coming about as a result of the fact that it has been ratified by 110 WTO Members, which pushes it above the threshold needed to take effect, namely ratification by two-thirds of the WTO's 164 Members.'[90]

— In conclusion:

- The volume and UK and EU will likely at least sign a basic goods FTA; meaning tariff-free goods trade will continue.

- The UK's rules and regulations are already synchronised with EU regulations and standards. This will also be true on the day after Brexit.

- The UK and EU are signed up to the WCO, which exists to help simplify and resolve customs issues.

- The WTO TBT agreement prohibits the EU from banning UK goods that meet international standards.

- The WTO agreement on Rules of Origin means that the EU will have to ensure rules of origin are administered "in a consistent, uniform, impartial and reasonable manner" when dealing with exports from the UK.

---

89   https://www.wto.org/english/tratop_e/tradfa_e/tradfa_introduction_e.htm

90   http://www.wcoomd.org/en/media/newsroom/2017/february/wco-welcomes-entry-into-force-of-the-wto-trade-facilitation-agreement.aspx

- The WTO Trade Facilitation agreement means the EU must co-operate with the UK on issues around the "movement, release and clearance of goods".

When we combine these factors together we see that after Brexit, UK trade with the EU will be very similar after Brexit as before Brexit.

The EU has signed up to many agreements and treaties which in effect reduce the uniqueness of the single market.

Britain can therefore essentially have almost duplicate trade relationship by falling back on these international agreements (if necessary) which would mean that the UK could have the majority of the benefits of single market membership, but be free to choose which rules to obey when not exporting to the EU 27 countries or for domestic sale.

The TFA might not then be the final nail in the single market coffin (it is still useful to EEA members), but it is one substantial step towards reducing the importance of the single market to a post-Brexit UK.

The EEA is not the answer on its own

Even if the UK and the EU were minded to keep Britain in the single market it does not of itself completely resolve all the post-EU trade issues that need to be addressed through effective negotiation.

Exports from an EFTA/EEA member must still go through a customs clearance process and outlay for VAT. These time-consuming procedures apply even to states such as Norway. Britain renouncing its EU membership but retaining, through membership of the European Free Trade Association, its status as a part of the European Economic Area will not on its own overcome the practical and bureaucratic trade hurdles. Norway, Iceland and Liechtenstein, the non-EU participants in the single market, do not enjoy true freedom of movement for goods.

Furthermore, the EU's application of time consuming rules does present opportunities for Britain. If a tariff free trade agreement is in place UK businesses can corner the profitable market for assembling goods. The now complex supply chains that dominate global production can create jobs in the UK.

Gateway Britain

Britain obtaining tariff free access to the remainder of the EU, along with measures designed to speed the passage of goods through customs, and developing trade links with the third countries around the world, will benefit Britain. Having a more liberal regulatory regime and tariff free access to the EU's single market will make the UK a base from which third country producers, who have entered preferential trade deals with Britain, can access the EU without being subject to tariffs.

Within Britain; value can be added to goods and re-exported from the UK to the EU. This will allow exporters to sidestep the EU's rules of origin regime. Britain will be able to become a regional value added production hub. The British economy will therefore not only benefit from the additional bilateral trade with other territories but will also capture a number of benefits:-

1. Increased trade

2. Increased freight and haulage through the UK as a pass through onto its final destination

3. Increased assembly and manufacturing within the UK (to meet rules of origin that require a declaration to be made that at least partial reworking has occurred to the produce)

4. Increased economic activity and employment and the resulting fiscal benefits

5. Increased use of a made in Britain mark makes the UK's regulatory regime more internationally relevant

Even in the EU, technical requirements on import processes as well as standards will differ from each country. However, the fear that EU legislation prejudicial to the UK may queer the pitch against British sales to the continent is probably unfounded.

As Britain conforms to EU standards at present there is little, if any, divergence. Further, as an increasing proportion of technical standards originate from global bodies, agencies of the United Nations, or relate to international agreements on technical barriers to trade, there will not be a sudden deviation from permissive regulations. These international agreements are designed to encourage cross border trade. It is worth reiterating the fact that rarely do customs officials demand compliance with standards and rarely do they conduct a strict examination of documentation declaring that an item conforms to national or EU standards.[91]

The strength of the UK's negotiating position

- Nearly 6 million EU jobs are linked with EU exports to the UK.

- The EU treaties advocate the EU to sign free trade deals, especially with neighbouring countries.

- The EU is restricted in what it can do to 'punish' the UK under the many WTO and WCO agreements it has signed.

- EU rules are increasingly being influenced by (or copies of) rules set by global or regional bodies.

- The UK is already harmonised with EU rules and the government has already pledged to repatriate existing 'EU Law' into UK law as part of the Great Repeal Bill, to minimise disruption.

- It is in the interests of the UK and EU to maintain close, friendly co-operation.

As Jaques Delors - Ex President of the European Commission notably said:

"The British are solely concerned about their economic interests, nothing else. They could be offered a different form of partnership.

"If the British cannot support the trend towards more integration in Europe, we can nevertheless remain friends, but on a different basis. I could imagine a form such as a free-trade agreement"[92]

The Good deal/Bad deal paradox

As we have outlined, there isn't much that European politicians can really do to punish the UK for leaving the EU.

---

91 Primary research with managers in the logistics industry

92 http://www.telegraph.co.uk/news/worldnews/europe/eu/9769458/Jacques-Delors-Britain-could-leave-the-European-Union.html

In any case, a bad deal for us is a bad deal for them, a good deal for us is a good deal for them. The European establishment know that as well as we do.

For diplomatic reasons, the UK could make a small concession to the EU. This would allow the EU to 'save face'. An example of this might be – the UK could agree to pay a few million pounds a year into the grants system that countries like Norway and Iceland administer; to off-set inequality between Western Europe and the post-communist economies of Eastern Europe.[93] In effect, these quite laudable grants are a form of foreign aid to European countries – and so the budget for them could come from the UK's existing foreign aid budget.

The UK can keep good will by continuing to partake in schemes such as the Erasmus programme. It does not mean that non-EU countries pay into the EU budget for accessing the single market. It is for services provided by the EU. These payments go towards research, the production of statistics, green programmes and charities, combatting cross-border organised crime including human trafficking, illegal immigration and smuggling amongst other issues.

Self-fulfilling Prophecies

Although the UK could trade and export outside both the EU and EEA (even with no FTA if necessary), certain sections of the media and disgruntled British politicians may attempt to present it as a 'doomsday scenario' for the British economy.

As we have seen before and after the EU referendum, any reports or comments in the media which appear to show the UK is heading for a 'Hard Brexit' have a temporary knock-on effect on the value of Sterling.

This is a classic example of the self-fulfilling prophecy. A group of MPs or business leaders make dire predictions about the economy, currency speculators take fright and the MPs or business leaders point to the ensuing drop in the value of Sterling as proof of their prediction, even though it was their prediction that caused it in the first place. Whilst also conveniently ignoring the fact that the drop in the value of the pound will drive exports and will ultimately help rebalance the economy. What is more, the drop in the value of the pound against the dollar drives up the value of the FTSE 100 index upon which many pension funds depend for their income.

A 'hard' Brexit is merely a media sound bite, it is a misnomer. There are procedures and agreements already in place that will protect trade and investment.

Final words:

"…with a bit of fancy diplomatic footwork and some political intelligence, the Government could negotiate retention of our membership of the single market along with curtailment of freedom of movement."

– Nick Clegg MP, former Deputy Prime Minister, former Member of the European Parliament[94]

Although this report demonstrates that the UK will survive outside of the EU and will suffer no major shocks from Brexit, Britain should not take any unnecessary risks.

---

93   http://eeagrants.org/

94   Hansard 12 October 2016

The government should approach negotiations in a spirit of friendship and diplomacy and sign a trade agreement (FTA) with the EU, containing specific agreements on product standards and financial services access.

These agreements would contain specific commitments to avoid non-tariff barriers and maintain services trade, building on the WTO, the TBT agreement and GATS. It should also contain references to minimising rules of origin and customs clearance issues.

During the Article 50 period, the UK should explore re-joining the European Free Trade Association, which incidentally Britain founded in 1960.

A UK-EU committee should be set up to monitor any new agreement between Britain and the remaining EU states. This is to resolve disputes and to ensure that the UK and EU continue to work closely together on trade and regional issues.

The UK will survive and thrive after Brexit, and in the words of MEP Dan Hannan:

"Brexit will change UK from the EU's 'bad tenants' to its 'good neighbours'."

APPENDIX

MoUs – the key to a smooth Brexit?

Whichever form Brexit eventually takes, whether 'hard' or 'soft'; most parties would like the transition to be as painless and smooth as possible.

To ensure that the Brexit process runs seamlessly, the UK and the EU countries could agree a time-limited *transition deal* as a temporary 'stepping stone' to the final outcome.

The deal need not be an official treaty but could take the form of what is called a Memorandum of Understanding or MoU.

As the UK government website states:

> 'An MoU records international "commitments", but in a form and with wording which expresses an intention that it is not to be binding as a matter of international law. An MoU is used where it is considered preferable to avoid the formalities of a treaty – for example, where there are detailed provisions which change frequently or the matters dealt with are essentially of a technical or administrative character; in matters of defence or technology where there is a need for such documents to be classified; or where a treaty requires subsidiary documents to fill out the details. Like a treaty, an MoU can have a variety of names and can also be either in the form of an exchange of notes or a single document. However, the formalities which surround treatymaking do not apply to it and it is not usually published. Confusingly some treaties are called memoranda of understanding. Although an MoU is not legally binding it should be no less carefully drafted than if it were a treaty, given that it is always the intention to perform all HMG's commitments, whether legally binding or not.'[95]

An MoU is an established device in public international law; less official that a treaty but more than a gentleman's agreement. MoUs can take various forms and can serve wildly different purposes. They can be short and cover one specific issue or be lengthy, covering a range of topics.

Examples include the Memorandum of Understanding on Trade and Investment (MOUTI) Between the Government of Canada and the Governments of Costa Rica, El Salvador, Guatemala, Honduras and Nicaragua[96] and the Memorandum of Understanding between the Council of Europe and the European Union.[97]

While they lack the legal certainty of treaties, the semi-official nature of MoUs means that one (or several relating to different areas of co-operation) could likely be signed quickly, without extensive consultation, parliamentary chicanery or ratification delays – as opposed to a potentially lengthy free trade agreement (FTA) ratification.

These interim documents could help avoid a potential 'cliff edge' scenario as the 2 year Article 50 period draws to a close in 2019.

---

95   https://www.gov.uk/government/uploads/system/uploads/attachment_data/file/293976/Treaties_and_MoU_Guidance.pdf

96   http://www.international.gc.ca/trade-agreements-accords-commerciaux/agr-acc/other-autre/ca-ac.aspx?lang=eng

97   https://eeas.europa.eu/sites/eeas/files/mou_2007_en.pdf

Once agreed, the document, or documents, should be signed by the Secretary of State for Foreign and Commonwealth Affairs on behalf of Her Majesty's Government, representatives of the European Council and European Commission (including the High Representative of the European Union for Foreign Affairs and Security Policy) on behalf of the EU and a representative from the EEA Council.

The text of the 'deal' should be officially sent to the FCO Treaty Section, The European Commission and The EEA Joint Council. We would then receive their signed copies in exchange, under the established procedure of international law called 'Exchange of Letters/Notes'.

As a sign of good faith, the MoU, signed by all parties, could then be deposited with the Secretary-General of the United Nations. This would not make the document any more or less binding, but it would be a show of good faith and would reassure businesses and concerned groups that all sides were committed to a stable transition. MoUs could therefore go a long way towards bridging the gap between our current EU membership and our final negotiated arrangement.

Below is a brief outline of what we believe the UK-EU MoU could look like.

DRAFT

Memorandum of Understanding

The purpose of this Memorandum of Understanding (hereinafter referred to as "MoU") is to maintain co-operation and secure free trade in goods and services between the signatories of the European Economic Area (EEA) agreement and the UK.

This MoU is intended to maintain where possible the *status quo ante* in terms of trade until a more permanent agreement can be reached between the Parties.

This Memorandum of Understanding is not legally binding on the Parties. This MoU is agreed in good faith between the signatories, on the basis that it is a fair and honest representation of their intentions.

Duration and Term

This agreement is intended to last for a period of two years from the date of signature. It may be renewed once, for a period of 12 months if all Parties agree.

Memorandum of Understanding on Trade and co-operation between the United Kingdom and the EU and EEA

BETWEEN THE UNITED KINGDOM OF GREAT BRITAIN AND NORTHERN IRELAND, OF THE ONE PART, AND THE SIGNATORIES OF THE EEA AGREEMENT:

[THE KINGDOM OF BELGIUM, THE REPUBLIC OF BULGARIA, THE CZECH REPUBLIC, THE KINGDOM OF DENMARK, THE FEDERAL REPUBLIC OF GERMANY, THE REPUBLIC OF ESTONIA, IRELAND, THE HELLENIC REPUBLIC, THE KINGDOM OF SPAIN, THE FRENCH REPUBLIC, THE REPUBLIC OF CROATIA, THE ITALIAN REPUBLIC, THE REPUBLIC OF CYPRUS, THE REPUBLIC OF LATVIA, THE REPUBLIC OF LITHUANIA, THE GRAND DUCHY OF LUXEMBOURG, HUNGARY, THE REPUBLIC OF

MALTA, THE KINGDOM OF THE NETHERLANDS, THE REPUBLIC OF AUSTRIA, THE REPUBLIC OF POLAND, THE PORTUGUESE REPUBLIC, ROMANIA, THE REPUBLIC OF SLOVENIA, THE SLOVAK REPUBLIC, THE REPUBLIC OF FINLAND, THE KINGDOM OF SWEDEN, ICELAND, THE PRINCIPALITY OF LIECHTENSTEIN, THE KINGDOM OF NORWAY], OF THE OTHER PART, hereafter jointly referred to as the "Parties":

RECOGNISING the longstanding alliances between the UK and the nations of Europe;

COMMITTED to renewing their close and lasting relationship that is based on common values, namely respect for democratic principles, the rule of law, good governance and free and fair trade;

DESIRING to maintain currently high levels of trade and investment and seeking to avoid future barriers to mutual trade and investment;

RECOGNISING that UK as a European country shares a common history and common values with the Member States of the European Union (EU) and the member states of the European Free Trade Association (EFTA);

RECOGNISING the importance of International trade and economic cooperation;

COMMITTED to combating organised crime and money laundering, to reducing the supply of and demand for illicit drugs and to stepping up cooperation in the fight against terrorism;

HAVING REGARD to the outcome of the 23rd June 2016 UK Referendum on EU membership;

BUILDING on their respective rights and obligations under the Marrakesh Agreement Establishing the World Trade Organisation, done on 15 April 1994 (hereinafter referred to as the 'WTO Agreement') and other multilateral, regional and bilateral agreements and arrangements to which they are party;

HAVE AGREED as follows:

CHAPTER I:
ARTICLE 1 DEFINITIONS

General definitions

For the purposes of this Agreement and unless otherwise specified:

GATS means the General Agreement on Trade in Services, contained in Annex 1B to the WTO Agreement

GATT 1994 means the General Agreement on Tariffs and Trade 1994, contained in Annex 1A to the WTO Agreement;

Parties means, on the one hand, the European Union or its Member States or the European Union and its Member States within their respective areas of competence as derived from the Treaty on European Union and the Treaty on the Functioning of the European Union (hereinafter referred to as the 'EU Party') and on the other hand, the UK;

TBT Agreement means the Agreement on Technical Barriers to Trade, contained in Annex 1A to the WTO Agreement;

TRIPS Agreement means the Agreement on Trade-Related Aspects of Intellectual Property Rights contained in Annex 1C to the WTO Agreement;

UK-EEA Joint Committee means the UK-EEA Joint Committee established under Article 5.1 (The UK-EEA Joint Committee);

Vienna Convention on the Law of Treaties means the Vienna Convention on the Law of Treaties, done at Vienna on 23 May 1969;

WTO means the World Trade Organization; and

WTO Agreement means the Marrakesh Agreement Establishing the World Trade Organization, done on 15 April 1994.

Article 2 Objectives

1. The Parties hereby establish a free trade area on goods, services, establishment and associated rules in accordance with this Agreement.

2. The objectives of this Memorandum of Understanding (hereinafter referred to as "MoU") are:

   (a) to liberalise and facilitate trade in goods between the Parties, in conformity with Article XXIV of the General Agreement on Tariffs and Trade 1994 (hereinafter referred to as 'GATT 1994');

   (b) to liberalise trade in services and investment between the Parties, in conformity with Article V of the General Agreement on Trade in Services (hereinafter referred to as 'GATS');

   (c) to provide appropriate protection of intellectual property rights, in accordance with the highest international standards, in conformity with The Agreement on Trade-Related Aspects of Intellectual Property Rights (hereinafter referred to as 'TRIPS');

   (d) to work to reduce non-tariff barriers between the parties, in conformity with the Technical Barriers to Trade ('TBT') Agreement;

   (e) to promote peace and security for all Europeans.

Article 3 Relation to the WTO Agreement and other agreements

The Parties affirm their rights and obligations with respect to each other under the WTO Agreement and other agreements to which they are party.

Article 4 Customs duties

No new customs duty on imports shall be introduced in trade between the EEA states and the UK. Parties shall not institute any new taxes or other measures having an equivalent effect imposed on, or in connection with, the exportation of goods to the territory of each other.

Article 5 Joint Committee - establishment

1. A UK-EEA joint committee is hereby established, which shall be responsible for the administration of the agreement and shall ensure its proper implementation. For this purpose, it shall make recommendations and take decisions in the cases provided for in the agreement. These decisions shall be put into effect by the contracting parties in accordance with their own rules.

2. For the purpose of the proper implementation of the agreement the contracting parties shall exchange information and, at the request of either party, shall hold consultations within the joint committee.

3. The joint committee shall adopt its own rules of procedure.

Article 6 Joint Committee - constitution

1. The joint committee shall consist of representatives of the EEA and its signatory states, on the one hand, and of representatives of the UK, on the other.

2. The joint committee shall act by mutual agreement.

3. The joint committee shall meet at least twice a year in order to review the general functioning of the agreement, with the meetings alternating between Brussels/Strasbourg and London.

4. The joint committee shall, in addition meet whenever special circumstances so require, at the request of either contracting party, in accordance with the conditions to be laid down in its rules of procedure.

5. Each contracting party shall preside in turn over the joint committee, in accordance with the arrangements to be laid down in its rules of procedure.

6. The joint committee may decide to set up any working party that can assist it in carrying out its duties.

Article 7 Political dialogue

1. The parties shall hold, by mutual agreement regular meetings at Foreign Minister level.

2. The parties shall take full and timely advantage of all diplomatic channels between the Parties, including within the United Nations (and specifically the UNECE), the Council of Europe, the OSCE and other international fora, to work towards resolution of shared problems.

3. Other procedures and mechanisms for political dialogue, including extraordinary consultations, shall be set up by the Parties by mutual agreement.

Article 7 Combating crime and terrorism

1. The Parties agree to work together at bilateral, regional and international levels to prevent and combat crime and terrorism in accordance with national and international law.

2. The main focus and instrument of this co-operation shall be via INTERPOL

3. The UK shall sign an operational agreement with EUROPOL

4. The Parties agree to co-operate closely via the United Nations Office on Drugs and Crime ('UNODC') and World Customs Organization (WCO).

5. The Parties agree to exchange information on terrorist groups and their support networks;

Article 8 Facilitating trade

1. The Parties agree to work closely on customs matters in order to facilitate legitimate trade and to ensure the integrity of supply chains.

2. The contracting parties also recognize the need for minimizing the incidence and complexity of import and export formalities and for decreasing and simplifying import and export documentation requirements.

3. The Parties agree to work closely to minimize difficulties caused by rules of origin (ROO) and that on the importation of products from the territory of a contracting party into the territory of another contracting party, the production of certificates of origin should only be required to the extent that is strictly indispensable.

Final Clauses

1. This Memorandum of Understanding may be amended by the written concurrence of all Parties.

2. The Memorandum of Understanding comes into effect upon signature and will remain in effect unless terminated by consensus. Any Party may withdraw from this Arrangement with previous written notification, twelve months in advance to the other Parties.

Authentic texts

This Agreement is drawn up in duplicate in the Bulgarian, Czech, Danish, Dutch, English, Estonian, Finnish, French, German, Greek, Hungarian, Italian, Latvian, Lithuanian, Maltese, Polish, Portuguese, Romanian, Slovak, Slovenian, Spanish, Swedish, Icelandic and Norwegian languages, each of these texts being equally authentic.

This agreement will be approved by the contracting parties in accordance with their own procedures.

Done at Brussels on the first day of May in the year two thousand and nineteen.

For the United Kingdom of Great Britain and Northern Ireland:

Für die Bundesrepublik Deutschland / For the Federal Republic of Germany:

Thar cheann Na hÉireann / For Ireland:

For the European Union / Pour l'Union européenne:

For the EEA Council:

THE BRUGES GROUP   ASSOCIATE MEMBERSHIP

TEL: +44 (0)20 7287 4414 | www.brugesgroup.com/join | info@brugesgroup.com

To join the Bruges Group, complete the following form and send it to the Membership Secretary with your annual subscription fee. This will entitle you to receive our published material for one year. It also helps cover the cost of the numerous Bruges Group meetings to which all Associate Members are invited. **You can also join online, right now, by using your debit or credit card. Please log on to www.brugesgroup.com/join or you can join over the phone by calling 020 7287 4414.**

Minimum Associate Membership Rates for 1 year UK Member £30 ☐ , Europe £45 ☐ , Rest of the world £60 ☐

Optional donation: £10 ☐ £20 ☐ £50 ☐ £100 ☐ £250 ☐ £500 ☐

Other, please specify: ....

If you are able to give more towards our work, we would be very grateful for your support. For the sake of convenience, we urge you to pay by standing order.

YES ! I wish to join the Bruges Group

Title: .... Name: ....

Address: ....

.... Postcode: ....

Telephone: ....

Email: ....

BANKERS ORDER Name and full postal address of your Bank or Building Society

To: The Manager:.. Bank/Building Society

Address: ....

.... Postcode: ....

Account number: .... Sort code: ....

Please Pay: Barclays Bank Ltd (Sort Code 20-46-73), 6 Clarence St, Kingston-upon-Thames, Surrey KT1 1NY

The sum of £ .... (figures)

Signature: .... Date: ....

to the credit of the Bruges Group A/C No 90211214 forthwith and on the same day in each subsequent year until further notice.

— or —

CHEQUE PAYMENTS I enclose a cheque made payable to the Bruges Group

The sum of £ .... (figures)

Signature: .... Date: ....

— or —

MEMBERSHIP PAYMENT BY CREDIT/DEBIT CARD

Solo ☐ Visa Card ☐ Visa Delta ☐ Visa Electron ☐ Mastercard ☐ JCB ☐ Switch ☐

Card number: ....

Valid from: .... Expiry date: ....Issue number: .... Security code: ....

Card holder's name as it appears on the card (please print): ....

.Address of card holder: ....

.... Postcode: ....

Telephone:..

Email: .... Signature: .... Date: ....

Please complete this form and return to:
The Membership Secretary, The Bruges Group, 214 Linen Hall, 162-168 Regent St., London W1B 5TB

www.brugesgroup.com

Honorary President: The Rt. Hon the Baroness Thatcher of Kesteven, LG OM FRS
Vice-President: The Rt. Hon the Lord Lamont of Lerwick **Chairman:** Barry Legg
Director: Robert Oulds MA **Head of Research:** Dr Helen Szamuely **Washington D.C. Representative:** John O'Sullivan, CBE
Founder Chairman: Lord Harris of High Cross **Former Chairmen:** Dr Brian Hindley, Dr Martin Holmes & Professor Kenneth Minogue